Sell with Soul

THE NEW AGENT'S GUIDE TO AN EXTRAORDINARY CAREER IN REAL ESTATE

Jennifer Allan, GRI

Bloomington, IN  Milton Keynes, UK

authorHOUSE®

AuthorHouse™
1663 Liberty Drive, Suite 200
Bloomington, IN 47403
www.authorhouse.com
Phone: 1-800-839-8640

AuthorHouse™ UK Ltd.
500 Avebury Boulevard
Central Milton Keynes, MK9 2BE
www.authorhouse.co.uk
Phone: 08001974150

First published by AuthorHouse 1/5/2007

ISBN: 978-1-4259-6882-3 (e)
ISBN: 978-1-4259-6881-6 (sc)

Printed in the United States of America
Bloomington, Indiana

This book is printed on acid-free paper.

Dedication

A huge thank you to my mother - Dorothy Allan - who has always been my biggest fan. We are so much alike...in ways we are just discovering. Thanks for reading to me every night and instilling in me not only love of the English language, but also a deep appreciation for using it right! Love you, Mom.

Sell With Soul

The New Agent's Guide to an Extraordinary Career in Real Estate

An Overview

You'll have a choice to make every day you sell real estate. To Sell with Soul... or with No Soul. Selling with Soul is not some new-age philosophy designed to help you discover your inner goddess, oh, no. It's a fresh approach to the art of real estate sales that shows you a new way, a better way to sell real estate and still respect yourself in the morning!

They don't teach you how to sell real estate in real estate school. In fact, very little training on competency is available at all. The failure rate for first-year agents is staggering, and it's not because selling real estate is all that hard. The chapter also includes some common myths, as well as some truths that may surprise you.

So much to do, so little time. Your first two items of business are building your Sphere of Influence (SOI) and learning your market. If you aren't obsessed (yes, I said obsessed) with these two projects, you will fail. Perhaps before you see even one paycheck. But don't worry! This will be fun!

This is a high-energy chapter - as in, have a good breakfast before you dive in. You'll find lots of information here about the buying process -- from pre-qualifying buyers to showing houses to making offers to preparing for closings, including fun topics such as "Are Buyers Really Liars?" and "Sign 'em up before you put 'em in your car." You'll learn how and why to control your emotions and why a premature discussion of buyer agency can chase off a new prospect. You'll be introduced to the first of many checklists. Finally, you will learn how to capitalize on your investor market and how to impress an out-of-town buyer.

Chapter Four: The Proper Care & Feeding of Sellers - Part I Page 83

Yahoo! You have your first listing appointment. Yikes! You have your first listing appointment! Never fear, we'll get you through it. I'll help you put together a professional listing presentation and guide you through the process of pricing the home. I'll help you through two of the most intimidating conversations in real estate sales -- discussing price with your listing prospect and negotiating your commission.

Chapter Five: The Proper Care & Feeding of Sellers - Part II Page 100

Market your listings like you care! Seriously, don't ever be accused of putting your sign in the yard and then vanishing until closing. Your sellers deserve better and I'll show you how to treat them right...from your MLS description to buyer feedback to virtual tours to open houses to flushing toilets. Negotiating good offers, bad offers, contingent offers or multiple offers. Two new checklists for you too!

Chapter Six: Negotiating Inspections from Both Sides of the Table Page 119

Depending on your market, the Inspection Provision in your real estate transactions can cut a new agent's income in half. I'd hate to see that happen to you. Negotiating inspections is a skill you'll want to develop as quickly as you can. I can help you with that.

Chapter Seven: Serving Your Client, Not Your Paycheck Page 127

In the heat of negotiations, it's easier than you might think to forget whom you represent (hint: it's not you). Your agency obligations, when not understood, can get you into a whole mess of trouble or, at the very least, embarrass you in front of your client. I'll give you some common agency pitfalls to watch out for, and then introduce you to the Open Checkbook Policy. You'll love it or hate it.

Chapter Eight: Special Types of Sales

This chapter is a bit of a yawn, so feel free to put it aside until you need it. Just don't forget it's here. Helpful advice and strategies for selling new construction and condominiums, and for dealing with FHA.

Chapter Nine: So You Want to be a Licensed Assistant?

No you don't. And here's why.

Chapter Ten: Some Final Thoughts, A Few More Stories & Last Minute Advice

You'll enjoy these random thoughts and anecdotes that didn't seem to fit in anyplace else, but I couldn't bear to leave them out. From getting over the heartbreak of being jilted to chasing down unearned referrals to painting your wealthy client's home, it's all in a day's work.

Random Reflections

Will your career be "extraordinary?" I hope so. Mine is and I'm grateful every day for the business of real estate that has made most of my dreams come true. Good luck!

Appendix

Contents

Welcome to Sell With Soul...
(Don't Skip This Section!)

You have a choice to make. Today. And tomorrow. In fact, you will make a very important decision every day you work as a real estate agent, from today until the day you retire from the business.

Each and every day, you'll have to choose between Good and Evil. Right and Wrong. Fair or Unfair. Respectful or Disrespectful. Every time you meet with or talk to a client...a prospect...a buyer...a seller...every time you make a judgment call or "executive decision" on a matter with no clear-cut answer... you'll need to choose on which side to hang your hat. The side with Soul... or No Soul.

What are some dilemmas you might face? Here are a few to ponder...will you pursue a referral fee from your brother's real estate agent? Should you encourage a bidding war on your brand new listing? Will you refuse to show your listing to a buyer who already has a buyer agent? Should you take advantage of the opportunity to learn an unfamiliar market with a new buyer? How much will you charge your first seller client? We'll discuss all these situations and many more – and you may be surprised by the "soulful" choices I recommend.

I'd like to tell you that if you make too many un-soulful choices, you will fail miserably in your real estate career. I'd like to tell you that, but I'd be lying (and that would be un-soulful!). Unfortunately, hundreds, if not thousands, of real estate agents have experienced wild financial success treating their clients and associates disrespectfully and...well, like dirt. This has not gone unnoticed by the general public; real estate salespeople "enjoy" a Top Five ranking in a

1

recent list of the nation's most *un-trusted* professions. Ouch! We're up there with car salesmen and politicians, a fact largely due (in my humble opinion) to what I call the "Old School" of real estate thought and training.

I'm sure you're familiar with the Old School philosophies. According to the Old School, the way to succeed in real estate is to treat it like a numbers game. To use condescending sales scripts, hard-core prospecting techniques and high-pressure closing strategies. Old School agents are frequently depicted in the movies as greedy, desperate, self-serving clowns. Unfortunately, these characters weren't invented by screen writers; they are alive and well and working in your neighborhood. And probably making a pretty good living.

But I'm guessing that if you purchased a book called *"Sell With Soul,"* you're hoping that there is a better way. A way to succeed without sacrificing your soul to do so. While you may freely admit that you want to make lots of money (and there's nothing wrong with that!), you'd prefer not to make it at the expense of your integrity or dignity.

Or, let's be blunt here, maybe you don't consider yourself particularly soulful (keep reading, you might change your mind!). But you doubt your ability to use the methods you've been taught by Old School trainers because they're just too "salesy" for you. You cringe when you imagine yourself making 100 cold calls a day, or putting those tired old closing techniques into play. You might even feel inadequate that you aren't overly enthusiastic about pestering strangers for business.

Quite simply, you know in your heart (and soul) that something is wrong with the advice of the Old School masters, yet you worry that you might not be successful unless you follow it.

Well, take heart—I have terrific news for you! You absolutely, positively <u>can</u> succeed in real estate sales without resorting to Old School methodology! And when I say succeed, yes, I mean you can make a ton of money, but oh, so much more.

A successful career in real estate can be a beautiful thing. An extraordinary thing. If you are a great real estate agent, that's something to be proud of. And chances are, if you are great, you will love your job. Can you imagine bouncing out of bed in the morning, every morning, eager to get to work? Or not dreading the end of your vacation because you're so excited about getting back to your business? Itching to check your voicemail messages because you can't wait to find out who called you while you were in the dentist's chair? If you've never experienced the euphoria of doing a job you love, and being well-paid to do it, ahhhh, you have something wonderful to look forward to.

With that, I welcome you to *Sell with Soul*. The *Sell with Soul* approach is radically different from the vast majority of real estate sales training programs out there. Selling with Soul centers around r-e-s-p-e-c-t. Respecting our clients – buyers, sellers, customers, prospects. Treating them like intelligent, competent human beings who don't need a lot of slick sales B.S. to make the right decision. Who don't need to be smoothly "closed" in order to sign the paperwork that secures our all-important paycheck.

To *Sell with Soul* means that we acknowledge and appreciate the generous "contributions" our clients make to our children's college educations (in the form of real estate commissions). That we are willing to part with a few of our precious commission dollars when it's the right thing to do. Especially when we screw up. But even when we don't. That we care more about the clients we have now than the clients we hope to have in the future. When our FOR SALE sign goes into a yard, we truly care about selling that home as much as our client does.

It means that when we forget to put our client first (it will happen), we at least feel bad about it. We might even <gasp> 'fess up and apologize.

When you *Sell with Soul*, you learn your job at your own expense, not at the expense of your paying customers, your buyers and sellers. You are competent. You know your market, your systems and your contracts. You are a good negotiator.

Not one of the tips, techniques, opinions or strategies found in this book is insulting or patronizing to your client. All my suggestions have clients placed firmly in first position, where they belong, and where your agency agreements (legal documents, remember) declare them to be. Sure, I'm irreverent sometimes, and rarely politically correct, but you'll find none of the hostility or cynicism toward your clients here that you may encounter elsewhere. Even in (especially in) your own real estate office.

* * *

I have a confession. Believe it or not, I'm naturally shy. Not wallflower shy, just...socially uncomfortable. Small talk is a foreign language to me. If I spend a day showing buyers around town or even holding a three-hour open house, I'll need some time alone to recharge afterwards. Cold calling or door knocking to prospect for business? You're kidding, right? You won't find me at any chamber of commerce networking event; heck, I get anxious about going to closings!

Not the best profile for a successful real estate agent, huh?

But I *am* successful! And not because I'm pushy, schmoozy or even particularly friendly. Just the opposite, in fact. Can I sell snow to Eskimos? Nope. Can I sell 75 homes a year? Yep. No problem.

I succeed in real estate, not because I'm charismatic, but because I'm Very Good at my Job. Good at the details, good at negotiating, good at the follow up. And no one is better than I am at creatively solving problems. Since I can't dazzle them with my charm, I have to blow them away with my competency.

I went into real estate on a whim, like so many others. My big plan was to get my license and make my fortune buying hot investment properties...maybe sell a few homes along the way (sound familiar?). I knew myself well enough to realize that I'd never be successful – after all, "the only way" to succeed in real estate is to knock on doors and dial-for-dollars, right? Well, that sure wasn't going to happen, so I figured I was out of luck. Hopefully enough friends would voluntarily hire me so I could pay the bills while I built my personal real estate empire.

But it didn't happen that way. Somewhere along the line I fell in love with my new career. I actually enjoyed selling real estate! No one was as surprised as I was when the sales results were tallied at the end of my first year, and I,

Jennifer *WayTooShyToSellRealEstate* Allan, was the second highest producing rookie out of 75 new agents. Okay, so I didn't set the world on fire, but I was doing something right. And believe me, it didn't involve calling up strangers or pestering By-Owner sellers.

This is not to say I didn't consider the traditional sales methods. Sure, I purchased and read all the guru books recommended to me...I say I read them...but I can't say I followed much of the advice I found within those sacred texts. Many of the techniques for cold calling, door knocking and farming left *me* cold and I sincerely doubted my ability to stick with programs that admittedly involved, even celebrated, cold hard rejection.

You've probably heard the philosophy...for every 100 phone calls you make, you'll get five appointments; for every five appointments you go on, you'll get one listing. Therefore, if you make 500 phone calls, you can count on five listings as a result. If your average listing commission is $5,000, then every phone call is worth $50 since it takes 100 phone calls to get a listing. The gurus claim you will actually start to enjoy each rejection, because you realize that every 99 "no's" equals a "yes" which leads to a paycheck, since every "no" means you are one step closer to a "yes." Sound fun?

For those of you who shudder at the thought of chasing down your prey, this book is for you. First, I'll help you build your business using respectful, non-invasive techniques. No farming, cold calling or door knocking. You won't have to hunt down For Sale by Owners (FSBO's) or Expired listings if you don't want to.

But more importantly, I'll help you to quickly develop the knowledge, skills and attitude to truly be an extraordinary real estate agent. An agent who, even during her rookie year, will inspire her friends to excitedly refer her to their friends and associates. When you're really, really good at your job, and you know it, confidence exudes from you. My clients laugh at me when I tell them I'm shy...more than once I've been told I'm one of the most confident people they know.

My professional confidence comes from *knowing* I'm a good real estate agent. Now put me in a room full of people who aren't interested in my real estate expertise and you'll find me hiding in the corner, slinking toward the exit as quickly and unobtrusively as possible. So, no, unfortunately, my professional confidence has never translated into social confidence. Ah well.

But I digress. *Sell With Soul* was written to help you build an extraordinary business using techniques and strategies that are far more respectful to your prospects and clients than the Old School methods. To help you develop the skills and expertise that will enable you to enthusiastically promote yourself and your services to the home-buying and -selling world out there.

So who am I...

...to give you advice on building a successful real estate business? Well, I'm not Tom Hopkins or Mike Ferry or Brian Buffini (names you have probably heard – if you haven't, you will). I haven't made a million dollars a year (yet) in real estate and I never had ten buyer agents working under me. I was not the top-producing agent in my city, nor did I ever qualify for any national lists of the most successful agents.

But I do well. Quite well. As mentioned, my first year I was runner up for Rookie of the Year and was later the perennial top agent in my office. My first full year in the business I earned around $70,000; my best year was $332,000. Today, I can easily count on $200,000 by working only eight months out of the year, four to six hours a day. Sound good?

My real estate career started off in the traditional fashion...go to school, pass the test, find a brokerage firm to hire me. But because I've always been a bit of a loner, by my second week I found myself working from home most of the time. By working from my home office, I missed out on the inevitable training-by-osmosis that occurs when you hang out in a busy real estate office...eavesdropping on the prospecting and closing techniques of other agents, watching the administrative staff process listings and closings, participating in the daily (hourly?) gripe sessions. I didn't get to listen in as the Top Dogs refused to negotiate their listing commissions, I didn't learn (from others) how to resolve a tough inspection. But neither did I waste all day Wednesday (tour day) with a bunch of other brokers who would never refer business to me.

I rarely saw my broker, so I was forced to solve my own problems, my own way. In other words, I developed my real estate expertise without a lot of distracting input from others. I might have recreated the wheel a few times, but overall, I feel that I created a better wheel and ran my business in a more professional, more creative and more client-centered fashion than many of the other agents I have run into.

About seven years into my career, after working from home all that time, I got the wild idea that I should immerse myself in the real estate culture and Go To The Office Every Day. Wow oh wow – my first experience in the real world of real estate. Sitting at my crummy desk, listening to the other agents use contrived sales scripts that were utterly condescending to anyone with intelligence, hearing the tired old listing and commission negotiating strategies ("No, I won't reduce my commission. If I can't hold firm negotiating for myself, how effective do you think I'd be negotiating for you?) The farming campaigns that (to me) were tacky and unprofessional. They worked, I guess, but it was hard for me to imagine putting my name on that garbage.

My experiment lasted about six months before I couldn't take it anymore. Although the other agents were a constant source of entertainment, I hadn't realized how mired in Old School tradition most of the real estate world still is. I was dismayed at the continuing blatant disrespect many real estate practitioners have for their clients and fellow salespeople. And the greed–oh my. But I'll talk more about that later.

WHY SELL WITH SOUL?

Lest you believe that I advocate the *Sell with Soul* approach only because I want to improve the reputation and public perception of the real estate industry, let me make one thing crystal clear. Selling with Soul will make you money. It might even make you rich. But not due to any universal cosmic karma. Not even because buyers and sellers will flock to your door 'cause you're so cool.

Sure, that will happen, especially as your referral business gains momentum, but, no, a big reason you'll make more money isn't just because you'll have more business. It's also because, by being soulful (i.e., competent, attentive and respectful), the real estate deals you work so hard to put together will close. Not only will you be able to recognize and solve the deal-breaking problems that threaten your paycheck every day, but as a soulful agent, you can keep everyone calm during chaos. People buying and selling homes get emotional, even irrationally so sometimes, and an out-of-control, ego-driven Old School agent often makes things worse.

Throughout this book, you will see many specific examples of Selling with Soul. You will see how a soulful real estate agent wields tremendous power over his or her business by simply being competent and following the Golden Rule. And that power is intoxicating. In a soulful way, of course.

If you believe, as I do, that a real estate transaction can be a win/win for everyone, and that at the end of the day everyone can still be friends, you have SOUL!

Sell with Soul. Be yourself. You don't have to be some hyped-up, blue-suited, smiley-faced "sales professional" to enjoy extraordinary success in real estate. You don't have to memorize scripts, make 100 cold calls or knock on stranger's doors. Unless you want to. Truly, you can wake up every morning, put on your own face and set the world on fire selling real estate. And enjoy every minute of it. Okay, most minutes.

Please Note...

The majority of my real estate experience, both personal and professional, has been in Colorado. Therefore, some of the terms I use may be unfamiliar to you if you work in a state with significantly different laws and practices. For example, Colorado is a table-funding state, which means that money exchanges hands at the closing table even though the documents have not yet been recorded. Sellers get their proceeds, real estate agents get paid, buyers get the keys. Some states, like California, are escrow states, which means there is no actual "closing" ceremony and funds are disbursed after all documents are recorded. When I use the term "under contract," it means essentially the same thing as "in escrow." I have tried to make my suggestions and instructions general enough to help you through the various processes despite minor or even major differences among markets. If something you find in this book sounds way off base, please check with your broker for clarification before putting my words into action!

Most of the names and events depicted throughout this book have been altered to protect the innocent and the not-so-innocent. Many anecdotes come from my own personal experience, but others have been gathered over the years from my friends and colleagues.

Jennifer Allan

1

What You Didn't Learn in Real Estate School
The Realities of a Career in Real Estate

So — Are You Ready To Sell With Soul?

Welcome to the Wonderful World of Real Estate Sales! You are about to begin (or have already begun) a career that can lead you to fame and fortune... or sadly be an unfortunate blip on the radar screen of your professional life. Statistics quote figures as high as an 80% dropout rate for first-year real estate agents and it's common knowledge in the industry that only 20% to 30% of the licensed agents are making enough money to live on...selling real estate, that is.

If you can get through your first year with your enthusiasm intact, you have beaten the odds and stand an excellent chance of success. And success in real estate is a beautiful thing. A career in real estate offers nearly unlimited potential for financial reward, an enviable lifestyle, and the opportunity to build an empire for your retirement or to pass on to your children. It can also guarantee you a captivated audience at social gatherings, if that's your thing.

Why is the failure rate so high? It's not as if real estate is brain surgery; there are thousands of non-rocket-scientist real estate agents out there making plenty of money. It's not a matter of supply and demand; there's plenty of business to go around, even in a slow market. Is it a matter of unrealistic expectations? Maybe. A lack of enthusiasm? Probably. A lack of support and training? Absolutely.

Funny, they don't teach you how to sell real estate in real estate school. They teach you how to pass the state exam. If you passed, they did their job. Moreover, the training provided by Big Name real estate companies is geared primarily toward teaching new agents to prospect, with little guidance on how to actually be a competent real estate agent.

But you may not be worried about that just yet, especially if you're brand new.

Brand new real estate agents have an arrogance about them (we all did) – especially if we bought or sold a few homes of our own in our past life. We think we know it all and are ready to take the real estate world by storm. Get out of the way, hot-shot agent coming through! Then reality creeps in. Our ignorance starts to show.

Maybe it happens when you're scheduling showings for your first buyer. Or when you're sitting down to write your first offer. Perhaps, like me, you panicked when you got your first listing under contract and had no idea what to do then. Or, also like me, when you stayed up 48 hours straight trying to put together your first market analysis. Most likely, all these scenarios will happen to you and provide periodic reality checks to keep you humble.

Or, perhaps, drive you screaming (or whimpering) from the business.

As a professional real estate agent, you are well paid for your services, and your clients expect you to be competent at your job, not just competent at prospecting. Your paying clients don't care if you have ten listings or two, if you have five upcoming closings or none. They do care deeply that you understand the real estate market, that you're a good negotiator and that you know how to look after them and their needs.

Most new agents learn the nuts and bolts of their business the hard way. Often at the expense of their paying clients and, consequently, at the expense of their own checkbook (if they're honorable). I'm going to try to help you avoid some of the costly or embarrassing mistakes, but believe me, you'll suffer your share of them anyway. Try to grin and bear it – it's true that you learn more from your mistakes than from your successes.

After six months or so in the business, you will have (hopefully) muddled your way through most of your "first times" and are feeling cocky again. Enjoy it – it won't last. The degree of difficulty of the challenges you encounter throughout your real estate career will increase in direct proportion to your experience and competency, always pushing you beyond your comfort zone. Just when you're feeling in control again, BAM! You'll be blindsided by an obscure FHA regulation or threatened with a lawsuit over a "non-conforming" bedroom.

Real estate transactions have many players, all of whom have their own (ever changing) rules of engagement. Most of these players are not interested in helping you learn their rules unless you show great promise and potential to make them money. Most (all?) new real estate agents are in "Fake It Till You Make It" mode for at least a year.

The Myths and Realities of a Career in Real Estate

When I think back to real estate school, it seems to me I remember a bunch of cocky, arrogant, middle-aged folks who were ready to set the world on fire. Real estate school was just a formality–they already knew it all. They smoked their cigarettes at break and regaled each other with grand stories of future riches and grandeur. Most of them were already "set up"– they were being sponsored by some hot shot broker or builder, or were going to be part of a fix-n-flip investment team and make a million in a few months. I don't think any of us thought we'd take the traditional route of building a real estate business from scratch.

Had you asked these students why they thought they would succeed in real estate, you'd have gotten a variety of answers. Since statistically it's likely most of them didn't succeed, we probably shouldn't give their opinions a lot of weight; indeed, most new agents have no idea what it takes to be successful, nor what to expect from a real estate career.

The general public's view of real estate agents is that we sit at open houses on Sunday and drive people around on Saturday. During the week, we look at more houses, just for fun. That's about it. When I decided to go to real estate school, all I knew about the job was what I had seen my real estate agent do and figured, heck, I could do that. Probably even better. That's what we all say.

Why do you think you'll be successful in real estate? Because you Love People and Love Houses? If you are successful, it won't be because you love people and houses. As the skeptics say..."Sometimes love is not enough." I never have particularly loved strangers and I was sick of looking at houses after about a year in the business. But I still enjoy my job and I'm definitely in that 20% of successful agents making a good living.

So, let's take a look at some of the myths you might be carrying around with you about the business of real estate and see if we can't shake things up a little bit for you.

MYTH #1
Your Love of People Will Make You a Successful Real Estate Agent

"She's not the friendliest person in the world, but she gets the job done" is how one of my biggest clients described me to a referral. After I picked myself up off the floor, I decided she meant it as a compliment, since obviously, she seemed satisfied with my service. And who am I kidding? No one has ever accused me of being a natural salesperson.

A general liking and appreciation for other people is a dandy characteristic for anyone to have, especially someone who has chosen sales as a career. But real estate isn't sales in the traditional sense. The only product you're selling is yourself; the rest of your job is primarily service related. If you are a people-person, great. It will help you be a successful real estate agent and possibly happier and more fulfilled overall. But if you're like me, with a natural tendency to shy away from social situations, don't fret. You can still be wildly successful in real estate.

But if, like me, you won't be able to distract them with your charm, you'll need to blow them away with your expertise. And responsiveness. And confidence.

I had a partner who was more of the warm fuzzy type. Whenever we tag-teamed a client (i.e., we both showed them homes or shared the listing), we always laughed at how she knew all the details of their personal lives and I didn't even know the ages of their children or what exactly the clients did for a living. I'm all business and don't mess around with small talk.

Not surprisingly, some clients loved her and disliked me, yet others preferred my efficiency and expediency. Different strokes. If you are the friendly type, you will attract and please a certain type of client. But if you're more like me – don't worry, there are plenty of "just-the-facts" real estate buyers and sellers out there who will think you're great. As long as you are good. I'm here to help you with that.

MYTH #2
Your Love of Houses Will Make You a Successful Real Estate Agent

This is probably the number one reason people choose real estate as a career. They loved the house-shopping process when they bought their first home and thought, "Gee, I could do this all day, this is fun!" And it is, at first. But after a year or two, the thrill is gone. You will know, from looking at a house from the street, pretty much what to expect on the inside. "Ah, a 1928 brick bungalow – narrow living room and dining room on the left, two bedrooms and a bath on the right, small kitchen in the back, stairs leading to the basement off the kitchen."

You'll get tired of struggling with jammed or frozen lockboxes. Your knees will scream in protest as you explore yet another two-story home with a finished basement. You'll despair as you realize that the owner of the home you're showing *is* home and intends to show you and your buyer every single closet personally.

I had a Ph.D. client (a special breed) who insisted on photographing every room of every house we looked at. Yes, even homes he had absolutely no interest in. Then he would take notes in his spiral notebook so he wouldn't forget what he'd taken pictures of. With approximate room measurements. Looking at eight homes with this guy would take far longer than the two hours I allowed.

While liking homes won't make you a success, having a working knowledge of home construction, your local architecture and a general idea of the cost of repairs just might. Your job as a real estate agent is not to Ooh and Aah over homes with your buyers, but to advise them on the issues that are important to them. Such as the cost to replace a 50-year-old furnace (the electrical may need to be upgraded and the chimney lined). Or that this particular lakefront neighborhood has a high water table, so we need to check out the sump pump. Or what to advise your buyer when a home smells like cat urine or cigarette smoke.

Maybe you'll never reach the point of buyer burnout, and if you don't, good for you. But don't go into real estate because you think you'll always enjoy a good day of house-shopping with your clients.

MYTH #3
You Have to Pester (er, Cold Call) Strangers to Build a Successful Business

Some people have it, some don't. The desire and willingness to cold call, door knock and network, that is. I'll bet many competent future real estate agents have been deterred from their calling, thinking that they had to spend their lives bothering people to get their business. Not true! I am living proof of that and so are countless other successful real estate agents.

Strangers may not be your best source of business anyway. Many real estate agents primarily prospect to strangers with newspaper advertising, web placement, bus bench ads, even billboards, but these self-promotion techniques are expensive. I've found that the agents who attribute their success to these techniques are the ones who could not pay the bills relying on a referral-based model. In other words, they don't get many referrals! Possibly because they are spending most of their time and energy on massive marketing projects rather than focusing on doing a good job for the clients they already have.

I've known many agents who operate this way. Their marketing efforts are legendary. They blanket their farm area with thousands of postcards, harass every expired listing, advertise on the radio and TV and pay big bucks for top placement on search engines. And they do get a lot of business, so I guess you could say these efforts are successful. But that's not the way I'd want to build my business.

(If the above sounds good to you, see if you can get a refund for this book. It won't be much use to you.)

It doesn't have to be that way. You can build a successful business on a combination of referrals and warm prospecting, which we'll discuss in depth later. Just know that if the thought of making a hundred phone calls a day asking the poor sap who answers the phone if he "knows anyone who's thinking of buying or selling real estate?" leaves you cold, don't for a minute think that you can't be as successful as you want to be.

MYTH #4
Your Job Is to Drive Buyers Around and Hold Open Houses
Because these are the most visible activities of a real estate agent, you may believe that this is pretty much what you do. Be grateful it's not! You'd die of boredom in six months. No, real estate is much more about problem solving, follow-up and customer service. These are the areas that will make or break your career.

MYTH #5
You Will Work Every Weekend
Surprise! You probably won't. Again, since you (and the general public) may think that your primary activities are open houses and showing houses to buyers, it's reasonable to expect that you'll work all weekend and rest on Monday. Not true. If you have a buyer or two, you may show them homes for a few hours on Saturday, but not as often as you think. If you do open houses (and you probably should), you may take up much of your Sunday preparing for and holding the open house.

But a major function of your job is to solve your clients' problems. The people who are going to help you do this work M-F 9:00 to 5:00. That's when you'll clock most of your hours. In your first few years, you may not have as much structured time off as you're used to, but you will certainly have plenty of time to do your laundry, your grocery shopping and even your workout. You just fit it in around the schedules of your clients. Real estate offers the Illusion of Controlling Your Time!

I hardly ever worked weekends. Why? Because Coloradans like to play in the mountains on their days off. They don't want to waste their Saturdays looking at homes, and if it's a good powder day at Vail, the phone doesn't ring at all.

MYTH #6
Real Estate Is a Team Sport

Real estate is an individual sport. Period. No one in your office or corporate headquarters cares much if you succeed or fail and, as you can imagine, there are always some who are rooting that you crash and burn. Regardless of any promises made during the recruiting full-court press, once you're on board, you're on your own in a lot of ways. It's up to you to succeed or fail. If you look as if you might succeed, you'll probably get a little more love from your broker and, if you're lucky, an experienced agent might take you under his or her wing. But real estate agents are naturally competitive and if they don't see any personal benefit to helping you out, they won't.

That said, you can find boutique offices that are more rah-rah and team-oriented and, if you're the

BROKER

When I reference "your broker" or "the broker," I am referring to the boss at your real estate firm. He/she is ultimately responsible for ensuring that you are trained and supervised and should be available to answer questions for you. He/she may or may not sell real estate along with managing the office. I also occasionally use the term "broker" to refer to other real estate agents as this is our proper title in Colorado.

type of person who needs the support of a team, you might try to search these out. I worked at one of these boutique firms for two years – lots of office activities – handing out candy at Halloween, pictures with Santa at Christmas, weekly office meetings, etc. All the agents in the office were good friends and frequently socialized together outside of work.

At this office, on Wednesdays (broker open house day), all the agents would travel around together to the open houses for the free lunches. Often they wouldn't get back to their desks (and their phone calls) until mid-afternoon. Friday evenings were frequently spent together at happy hours and every month at least one agent had a little soiree for the other agents in the office and their spouses.

As you may have noticed by my use of "they" in the preceding paragraph, I did not participate. To me, it was crazy to spend what little free time I might have socializing with other real estate agents – how much business are they going to send my way? This is a business of constant prospecting, and your friends should be your primary source of good referrals. Any social activity you do should be a potential source of business, even if you don't overtly prospect.

If you must, have one or two friends in the business to brainstorm and commiserate with, but don't make your colleagues your main source of friends. There are only so many hours in the day; don't waste good prospecting time hanging out with the competition.

Was I popular at this rah-rah office? What do you think?

Did it bother me? Sometimes.

But, who do you think was the top producing agent?

MYTH #7
You Shouldn't Ever Discount Your Fee

I will discuss fee negotiation in depth later in the book, but, contrary to popular opinion, I think you can find perfectly acceptable reasons to discount your fee. And not just because you capitulate to the pressure of the seller at your listing presentation. I think discounting your services for your friends and past clients is a great idea, as is offering a deep discount while you're learning the business. That said, you can actually avoid any discussion of fee negotiation, which is often the most painful part of your listing presentation. (I'll show you how in Chapter Four.) When you should be discussing the price of the home, your proposed marketing activities and your enthusiasm for the property, instead you're battling with the seller over your commission percentage. This is not the way to build trust or rapport between you and your seller, which will be critical during the process of marketing and selling her home.

But anyway, don't get all snotty about reducing your fee in the right situation. There's plenty of money to go around, so don't be greedy!

Some Truths

Successful real estate agents can make big bucks. For a career that requires only a month or two of education, the rewards can be tremendous. But be aware of the reasons the economy supports paying real estate agents such high fees.

One of them is that you are not a nine-to-fiver. You are available! Most of the world works nine-to-five; therefore, as a service provider (that's what you are), you need to be available when it is convenient for your clients. If you want to work regular hours, think about working for a builder as an on-site salesperson.

Don't get me started on those real estate agents and real estate coaches who refer to themselves in the same context with CPA's and attorneys. Such as..."You wouldn't call your CPA at 7:00 on Sunday evening..." or "You wouldn't try to negotiate your fee with your attorney, would you?" Get over it, people.

Tirade Alert!

WE ARE REAL ESTATE AGENTS, NOT CPA's. COMPARE THE EDUCATION AND LICENSING REQUIRED TO GET YOUR JD, MD OR CPA AGAINST THE MONTH OR TWO YOU SPEND IN REAL ESTATE SCHOOL LEARNING HOW TO PASS A ONE-HOUR TEST. IF I WERE GOING TO BE SO ARROGANT AS TO COMPARE MYSELF TO ONE OF THESE PROFESSIONALS, I WOULD MORE LIKELY USE AN OBSTETRICIAN AS A COMPARISON. WHEN THE BABY IS READY TO COME OUT, THE DOCTOR GOES TO WORK. EVEN AT 7:00 ON SUNDAY EVENINGS.

The good news is that successful real estate agents can make as much as or more than these higher qualified professionals, but with some trade-offs.

First, you need to be available to your clients when it's convenient to them, not you. Sure, they'll take time off from their work-day to visit their attorney, but they may not do it for their real estate agent. If you insist on working

M-F -9:00 to 5:00, believe me, someone else working evenings and weekends would be happy to take your prospects. And they will.

Second, you agree to be paid on contingency. You take the risk every day that the work you do will not be compensated. More Risk = More $Reward$. Less Risk = Less $Reward$. Not too many professions work with no guarantee of payment. Therefore, you can justify higher fees upon success. If you could convince your clients to pay you hourly (good luck), you could charge a reasonable hourly fee and would probably make much less money per transaction. Overall, you might come out ahead though.

So remember that the next time you get a $10,000 paycheck for, say, ten hours of work–that $10,000 is also paying for those flaky buyer clients who run you around and mysteriously disappear. It doesn't mean that you and your services are worth $1,000/hour.

We real estate agents get spoiled by our big paychecks. We actually think we earned that $10,000 check during that specific transaction. Even if a client put you through the wringer for a year, it's not likely you spent more than 50 hours on his transaction. And, $200 an hour is pretty good pay for anyone.

My personal mantra is that "I sell real estate every day. Sometimes I get paid for it, sometimes I don't." It keeps me sane!

So before you get hostile toward prospects who never take you to a closing, realize that real estate fees are structured to pay you for that "wasted" time. Of course, the better your closing ratio, the less you have to worry about such things, but in your first year(s) you will "waste" a lot of time on unproductive people. But, as we will see later, there is no such thing as wasting your time in your rookie year.

First Things First ∼ Some Thoughts on Choosing Your Office

If you haven't yet selected a real estate office to bless with your presence, here are some ideas to ponder.

Be assured that there is a place for you. If you are marginally presentable looking and have a pulse (most days), a real estate office will "hire" you.

In fact, the interview process is more about you interviewing them, rather than the other way around. Big Name companies specialize in recruiting and training new agents fresh out of school and will be happy to talk with you. You might even feel a little flattered at their attention and persuasive recruiting tactics!

That said, smaller boutique companies don't typically recruit rookie agents. If they do, they tend to be quite selective, so if you prefer to start your career at a boutique firm, you may have to actually sell yourself to the broker. Brokerages in small towns or resort communities may also be a little harder to break into than those in a metropolitan area.

When I first got my license, I was told that the urban brokers (where I wanted to work) wouldn't even talk to brand new licensees. Being shy, I didn't push the issue, I just interviewed in the suburbs and received "offers" from every suburban company I talked to. I chose to work in a Big Name office in the foothills outside of Denver because it sounded glamorous to sell mountain real estate. Never mind that I knew nothing about mountain real estate, or cared, really. I couldn't relate to the other brokers in the office or to any of the prospects I gathered who wanted a mountain lifestyle. I was a city girl and I understood city dwellers.

After nine months, I transferred to another office in a suburb of Denver. That was an even worse fit for me; while I didn't really connect with mountain buyers, I was utterly baffled by suburban ones! Tri-level homes built in 1975 with popcorn ceilings just weren't my thing. Six months later, I moved again, this time to a boutique firm in central Denver. Ah, the euphoria and camaraderie of working with agents who knew the difference between a Bungalow and a Cottage, a Denver Square and a Victorian.

My point is that you should strive to work in an office that fits your personality and interests, whether it is a specific neighborhood or market, an age group, a market specialty or just general ambience. Some offices are quite formal and stuffy; others are somewhat casual or even dumpy. You'll find corporate firms to be beige, boutiques more colorful and eclectic. Opportunities for referrals and good open houses will come more naturally (and be more enjoyable) if you are working in an atmosphere that feels like home. You will probably "know" when you're in the right place. Wait for that feeling.

However, don't fret if your first office doesn't work out. It's no big deal to move and, after a year in the business, you'll have a much better idea of what you're looking for.

A Word About Splits

As you probably know, your split is the percentage of your commissions you get to keep. If you are on a 60/40 split, you keep 60%, your brokerage firm gets 40%. When you're brand new, there probably isn't a lot of room to negotiate the split and you'll drive yourself crazy trying to compare offers from different companies. Just select the company that seems to best suit your personality, your need for training and/or personalized mentoring and, of course, your budget. You can worry about negotiating a better split after you've proven yourself.

Ready to Begin?

The goal of *Sell with Soul* is to go beyond helping you "survive" your rookie year, although with the staggering first-year failure rates, survival alone might be a worthy goal. But, no, I want to go much further than that. I'd like to help you lay the foundation for an extraordinary career selling real estate. By developing healthy habits early on, you can create a career that will not only pay the bills (quite nicely), but also provide a lifestyle for you and your family that the paycheck-to-paycheck world only dreams about.

But that's a few weeks off at least. You have some hard work ahead of you, so let's get started.

2

Let's Get This Party Started!
So much to do, so little time...

Building Your SOI, Learning Your Market & Finding Your Team

ENTHUSIASM

You must have enthusiasm to succeed in real estate. It's so easy to procrastinate when you are self-employed – or to sleep late every day if you're so inclined. Prospecting and previewing seem thankless sometimes.

When I was new in real estate, I had it – enthusiasm, that is. I did open houses every weekend, took names and made cookies. I would work with any buyer, regardless of his motivation or time frame. I even offered to show relocating *renters* around town just in case they might buy a house someday. I marketed my listings in every imaginable venue—newspapers, mass mailings, postcards and city-wide brochure distribution.

I answered the phone at all hours of the day or night. I worked seven days a week. I checked voicemail during vacation and returned business calls from a hot, noisy street in Mexico.

I'm not saying that these were all smart things to do – I spent a lot of money unnecessarily and destroyed my marriage in the process. But to succeed in this tough business you need to be excited about your new career, nearly to the point of fanaticism.

I once interviewed a licensee right out of real estate school who announced to me that he intended to take every Sunday and Monday off. Fair enough. But then I realized that he meant he wouldn't even answer his phone on his days off, at the risk of losing potential customers. After several years in real estate, I got to the point where I was willing to risk losing customers for the sake of a mental health day, but in my first year? No way. I lived for phone calls from potential clients. I literally did cartwheels a few times when I got off the phone from a new buyer or a referral. I got a little thrill every time my pager went off; I couldn't wait to see who had called. I still feel that way most of the time.

That new agent didn't make it in real estate – he quit within the year. He probably could have been a great agent, but his heart just wasn't in it.

If your lifestyle doesn't accommodate a 24/7 availability to your clients, you can still succeed. You can always find people willing to work harder than you, regardless of what field you are in. And guess what? They may be more successful financially than you, and that's fair. Life is about priorities and compromises. You can't have it all and do any of it exceptionally well. That said, early in your real estate career you really do need to be committed to building your expertise and business. Remember the 80% failure rate for first-year agents? An awful lot of those failures are likely competent people who aren't prepared for the overwhelming demands of a new real estate career.

Just think about it.

A $7,000 Phone Call

Back to the issue of 24/7...as part of my research for this book, I read several "How to Succeed in Real Estate" books. I found that I disagreed with much of the advice I found, especially the advice to "work regular hours." As in, don't take calls after 6 p.m., don't work seven days a week, don't drop everything to meet your client in 15 minutes.

Okay, sure, follow that advice if you have plenty of money, plenty of experience and no enthusiasm for your career. Are you telling me that you aren't dying for the phone to ring? If you aren't, you may be in the wrong business.

As a rookie agent, you probably aren't all that busy. At least, you aren't busy doing activities that are bringing in a paycheck in the next 30 days. When the phone rings and a prospect wants something from you, you better respond.

One Sunday evening early in my career I was putting dinner on the table for my husband and his parents. My cell phone rang. I love my job, so it didn't occur to me not to answer it. Turns out it was a buyer I had worked with six months earlier who hadn't bought anything. She and her husband were open housing that afternoon and stumbled upon a home they had to have. And, God bless 'em, they called me! If I hadn't answered the phone, their next call would have been to the agent holding the open house and I never would have known.

I dropped everything, wrote up the offer, and made $7,000 because I answered the phone. This happens, a lot. If your lifestyle doesn't allow you to be this responsive, maybe now isn't the time for you to go into real estate. However, when you're real successful, several years down the line, you may decide your personal life can't take being on call 24/7. At that point, it may be acceptable to forego a $7,000 commission, but in the beginning, I assume it would break your heart to miss a call like this.

Do you get excited when the phone rings?

* * *

Okay, enough with the niceties. The first two items of business to jumpstart your career are:

√ *Building Your SOI*
√ *Learning Your Market*

Oh, sure, you can find lots of other things to be doing, but these are by far the most important. Without the first, you have no one to sell to. Without the second, you have nothing to sell.

BUILDING YOUR SOI

Make a list of everyone you know. This is one of the first, if not the first, duty your new broker will give you. And that's good advice. G' ahead and do that.

SOI

Sphere of Influence = People Who Know You

How many people do you have on your list? 25? 50? Doesn't really matter. Just make the list and make your broker happy. If you're technologically inclined, you should put this list on your computer–I use Top Producer, but many other programs are available. Chances are, you're already using some program to keep track of your friends and family. That'll do for now. This may not be the best time to learn (or avoid learning) some fancy new program anyway. Now is the time for action and productivity, so don't get bogged down trying to figure out a complicated contact manager program. Unless that's your thing; if so, go for it.

Once you're "in real estate," your antennae will go up and your list will start growing like crazy. Everyone you meet will be added to your SOI. If it isn't happening naturally, start training yourself to think this way. Set your own goals–maybe you want to add five people a day to your SOI, or 15 people a week. Whatever works for you. Make it a game. Get names, addresses, email addresses (critical) and phone numbers. It's really important.

Before I was in real estate, I only had a few friends, by choice, I liked to believe. I've just never been the type to need a lot of people around me. As you know, I am shy and was reluctant to impose my friendship on anyone. Asking a friend or client out for drinks took a lot of courage for me. In fact, I was reprimanded several times in my last "real" job because too many of my clients complained that I didn't socialize with them.

My point is that I was too shy to aggressively turn acquaintances into friends. As soon as I got my real estate license, that changed. Call me opportunistic, but I began to see friendships in a whole new light. Instead of shying away from social opportunities, I began to seek them out and nurture them. It was a life-changing realization for me. I still remember the amazement I felt when

I invited some new(!) friends over for Thanksgiving dinner and they happily accepted. And actually showed up!

So, if you're shy like me, real estate can help change that. If you're already a people-person, you'll just need to train yourself to always be in SOI-building mode. You'll be amazed how quickly your list will grow to 100, 200, even 300 names. Don't let this list get stale and outdated. Make a promise to yourself to keep it current and it will be like gold to you.

Four Easy Strategies for Building Your SOI

1. Take Your Friends to Lunch

On my first day as a licensed sales associate, I went to a motivational seminar with my new broker. I don't remember what the seminar was about, but one particular point made by the speaker has stuck with me all these years. He called it Fishing from the Friendly Pond. It goes something like this:

When business is a little slow and real estate agents get hungry, they automatically want to ratchet up their advertising. They run newspaper ads, consider advertising on bus benches, do a mailing. They go "Fishing in the Unfriendly Pond" (i.e., strangers). Maybe the additional advertising will work, but more likely it will just be a write-off at tax time.

What agents should do (all the time, not just when it's slow) is "Fish from the Friendly Pond." Your friends, your family, your past clients. They care about you (at least more than strangers do) and are much more likely to try to help. Do you know 50 people? No? 25? Sure you do. If 25 people tell 5 friends about you, that's 150 people (your 25 friends + their 125 friends) who know you're in real estate. If those 125 friends of friends mention your name just once, you have 125 more potential clients. So, we're up to 275 people working on your behalf.

That's the Friendly Pond theory. Direct your prospecting efforts toward the people who care about you, not people who have never heard of you.

That sounded good to me. Better than cold calling anyway. So, during my first year, I took all my friends to lunch. Simple enough. Friendly lunches, not trying to sell myself or anything like that. ***And, I swear, I got a client and usually a closing from every single lunch.***

After my first year, I was too busy for my take-my-friends-to-lunch campaign. Sure, being busy is a good thing, but it was a mistake on my part to abandon this incredibly successful prospecting tool. Don't make the same mistake.

CLOSING

Closing is the consummation of the real estate transaction, when the seller formally delivers title to the buyer in exchange for payment of the purchase price. In some regions, all parties attend the same closing. In others, the buyer and seller close separately.

I saw the magic in action from the other side recently. I purchased a second home in Alabama and my real estate agent took me to lunch to thank me for my business. During our conversation, she mentioned a great little house she'd recently shown that she was considering buying as an investment. My ears perked up and I said I might be interested if she wasn't. She showed me the house the next day and I bought it, as well as another one right down the street. So, just for taking me to lunch ($11.48), my agent made nearly $10,000 in commissions! Well, not quite–I got a 25% referral fee from her for both homes because I'm in the business–very cool. Anyway, you never know who among your friends has money to spend on real estate and/or knows someone who does.

By the way, here's something fun to do that I wished I'd done from the beginning: keep a list of everyone you have lunch with. Every year or so, look at the list and see how many sales you got, either directly or indirectly, from these lunches. I think you'll be surprised.

I found that the majority of my early business (over 50%) stemmed from just one social encounter I had my first year. I met David (an agent from Aspen) at a continuing education class and we went to lunch during the break. He referred me to Brian, who was looking for investment properties in Denver. Brian referred me to Steve, who was selling his house next door to Brian and was also an investor. While listing one of Brian's fix-n-flip townhouses, I met Chris, who was looking for fix-n-flip properties and was a custom home builder. While showing Steve a duplex downtown, I met Deborah, the seller of the duplex, who was an out-of-state real estate agent looking for someone to refer business to in Denver. Deborah referred me to Samuel, who referred me to Ken, who referred me to....you get the point.

Just from that one lunch with David-from-Aspen in 1996, I made over $150,000.

Brian	12 Sales	$43,000
Steve	8 Sales	$28,800
Chris	7 Sales	$30,240
Deborah	5 Sales	$21,600
Deborah's referrals	10 Sales	$43,200

Put this book down and go schedule three lunch dates! Right now.

2. Get Out of the Office

I am a homebody. Someone once called me a high-functioning hermit. If I could sell real estate and never leave the house, I'd be a happy woman. But, alas, prospects and future paychecks do not come knocking at my door (although they do come across my Outlook Express).

Go do something where you will bump into other people. Just be out there in the world, with your antennae up. Do you have a friend who works at or, better yet, manages a restaurant? Drop by for a salad. Or take your dog to a dog park. If you're single, think of all the hot spots for meeting other singles; they might work for real estate prospecting too. Drop in on your favorite mortgage broker just to say hi.

One source for prospects can be the sales office of a home builder. As long as you have a legitimate reason to be hanging out there, you'll be surprised at the contacts you can make. One year I sold several units in a new townhouse community and bought one for myself, so I found myself visiting the sales office often for various reasons relating to my sales. The sales staff knew me and were comfortable with my presence there. When interested buyers came into the sales office, I'd find myself chatting with them myself about the builder's project and real estate in general. Please note, I did not try to steal away their business from the sales agents, I was really just making conversation. I listed more than one home from contacts I made at the builder's sales office and if nothing else, always walked away pleased for getting my shy self and my market knowledge out there in the public.

If the real estate market is strong, you'll have no problem finding an audience for your market expertise and professional opinions. Baseball games, concerts in the park, barbecues, weddings–anywhere people congregate and converse with others–are great places to casually start up a conversation about real estate.

3. My Low-Tech PDA

In my first year, I had a little system that worked surprisingly well for me. Index cards. I carried around a stack of cards, wrapped in a rubber band. Whenever I talked to someone about real estate, I wrote down his or her name and contact information on one side, and on the other, his real estate need or interest. Pretty simple.

I'd go through the cards every few days and follow up with the prospects as appropriate. I was always surprised at how quickly I'd forget about these prospects and realized that without the cards, many, many potential clients would have been lost forever. I stopped using the cards at some point and I sometimes wonder how many dozens of sales I missed because I inadvertently blew someone off.

Maybe $100,000 worth? Easily.

4. Be the First One to Call Back

Once you have a little momentum, your phone will start to ring. Carry a cell phone and a pager - and use them. When buyers are hot to buy a house, they are calling agents all over town. The first agent to call back and act as if they want the buyer's business will get the buyer's business. In my first year, this was a huge factor in my success. I was always the first agent to call back and was always cheerfully ready and willing to show the buyer whatever he or she wanted to see. Did I waste a lot of time with lookie-loo's? Sure. But did I sell more houses than the other rookies in my company? Yep.

I am just as responsive with e-mail, even more so. Internet-savvy buyers (and most are these days) aren't patient sorts. If they e-mail you with an inquiry, they'd really like an answer before they log off the computer for lunch. Sooner, if possible.

If you can't or won't respond to Internet inquiries, find someone to refer these leads to. Many times these prospects will vanish into cyberspace, but really, how much time does it take to acknowledge and respond to an e-mail? Maybe 45 seconds? If you send them some listings, maybe 15 minutes?

So my point is - you have a great chance at snagging some good buyer clients if you seem eager to help them. If you're the first one to respond, either by phone or e-mail, with some enthusiasm in your voice, you're already miles ahead of your competition.

What Didn't Work for Me

Because I was so enthusiastic about my new career, I tried it all. And wasted an incredible amount of money. I did a lot of mailers, from boilerplate newsletters to "Spring Forward" postcards to Just Listed/Just Sold announcements. I think I got one new client in ten years from all my mailings, and that was someone I went to high school with who recognized my name from a Bronco's football schedule I sent out. I also prospected expired listings with a custom postcard campaign I designed myself and was pretty proud of - and I got one listing that expired again because the seller simply wasn't motivated. One year I spent $20,000 on newspaper ads that resulted in - zero phone calls. Zero! Once I spent $1,000 on a catered broker luncheon for a $500,000 listing and only 15 agents showed up. I spent one Saturday evening sticking open house flyers under the windshield wipers of cars parked at a church and no one came to the open house anyway.

Let's see, what else? I advertised on bus benches, created beautiful custom magnets, sent out annual calendars and Christmas cards, even offered a lottery for a "Free Listing" one year. None of these efforts were noticeably effective. Getting your name and business card Out There in the World is important, but in the beginning, you really shouldn't be spending your precious marketing dollars this way. I know you feel helpless at times and just want to be doing something productive - so go preview, take a friend to lunch, go to the dog park.

Or - the absolute best business generating technique - are you ready? Plan a vacation. I guarantee that the week before you leave will be the busiest week of your life. Ask any experienced agent. It's foolproof.

* * *

Truthfully, I built my business on four simple techniques. Taking my friends to lunch (huge), getting out in the world with my antennae up, following up on my index cards and being the first to call back. I also held open houses, sat on floor time and did a little farming, but I don't have any great success stories to share with you from those activities. I remember being bored and discouraged though, which is the last thing you need while you're trying to build momentum. Nothing generates additional business like being too busy to handle more business.

> **JENNIFER'S $0.02...**
> *I have mixed emotions about open houses, and you will no doubt sense my ambivalence toward them throughout this book. There are good reasons to do open houses, the most important of which is that your sellers will expect you to. Open houses serve many functions for the real estate agent, and in time, you will decide for yourself how they fit into your business plan. Later in this chapter we will discuss open houses in some detail, as well as in Chapter Five.*

I'll leave you with one more bonus strategy - when you're busy, go look for more. I know you'll be feeling overwhelmed, but that's the best time to prospect. You'll be glowing, with enthusiasm oozing out of every pore. Your attitude will be irresistible and the universe will respond with even more business for you.

Just don't whine about how busy you are, either to yourself or to anyone else. It's irritating and self-defeating. Practice saying, "Business is unbelievable - I never thought I'd enjoy real estate so much!"

Learn Your Market

A few years ago I considered moving to Florida. Tired of the Colorado snow, I made an exploratory trip with the goal to see if Florida felt like "home" and, if so, could I afford to live on or near the beach?

I had never shopped for real estate in Florida and had no familiarity with the market. I walked into a real estate office in Ft. Lauderdale and asked for the agent on floor duty. Judy Johnson offered to help me. I told her my story and gave her my general price range. I told her I wanted to live near the beach, hoping she wouldn't laugh at me (I didn't know the market, maybe I was asking for the impossible). She didn't laugh, which was encouraging - she just said, "Well, let's just go over to the computer and see what's available."

Judy struggled a bit with the computer. She couldn't seem to get the MLS system to load, and when it did, she had trouble identifying which MLS areas near the beach fell into my price range. She did her first search, which turned up nothing. She said, "Oops, I accidentally asked for co-ops, not condos." She ran her search again, and turned up eight properties. She couldn't figure out how to access the additional pictures of these eight properties.

> **JENNIFER'S $0.02...**
>
> *It's a good reality check for you, as a real estate agent, to see what it feels like on the other side. You will be reminded how vulnerable and dependent on you your clients are, especially when they are new to your area.*

MLS

Multi-List System. The online database of properties listed for sale, as well as well as historical data on homes sold, expired and withdrawn from the market.

As it turned out, none of the properties were that close to the beach anyway, and most were age restricted - i.e., the buyer had to be at least 55 years old.

After almost two hours of this, she printed out listings for several condos and houses (don't ask about the struggle with the printer), gave me a map and asked me to drive by the homes. I was worn out, hungry and much less enthusiastic than I had been two hours ago. I headed out, map and listings in hand, fully intending to do my drive-by's. Instead I ended up stopping at Denny's for lunch and driving back to my hotel for a nap, frustrated and unhappy with Ft. Lauderdale.

Two days later, I wandered across Alligator Alley and found myself in Naples, Florida. I walked into a Re/Max office and talked to the agent on floor duty, Jim Peterson. I told Jim my story and this was his response:

"Well, Jennifer, if you want to live right on the beach, you'll definitely be looking at a high-rise condo. Prices for beachfront two-bedroom condos start around $400,000. Your monthly HOA dues will run anywhere from $300/month to $600/month. Some allow pets, but most don't. Now, if you're willing to live three blocks from the beach, we can find you a townhome for around $300,000. If you really want a house, we can get you within two miles of the beach, but anything closer will be over a million. Let me show you some of my favorite projects and see what you think."

Whew, didn't that feel better? Don't you think I felt much better cared for? Doesn't this agent sound like the one who can make my dreams of beachfront living come true? Or not, as it turned out, since my dream of a beachy home was out of my price range. But wasn't it better to know that in five minutes rather than two hours?

Jim was just doing his job. Our job as real estate agents is to know the market (and our systems!) better than our customers. We are well paid for our knowledge as well as our ability to share that knowledge with our customers. In this age of technology, any fool can pull up information on the properties for sale; it's our job to efficiently match that data with the person sitting in front of us.

Your product is property. Whatever your specialty is - single family homes, condos, vacation rentals, vacant land, new homes, old homes, ugly homes - you should know more than your audience about your product. As a newer agent, you can't call on experience you don't yet have; your experience level is beyond your immediate control. What you can control is your knowledge of your market.

Three Ways to Learn Your Market FAST

1. "Preview with a Purpose"

The best way I know of to increase your product knowledge is to preview. Previewing means scheduling appointments to look at listed properties without a buyer. Get out there and start looking at homes! But, if you're like me, previewing without a real purpose is a waste of time. I need a reason to preview that makes the information I glean "stick" with me.

So, come up with a purpose for your previewing. One great way is to preview around an open house you're doing next Sunday. Since you may not have any listings of your own yet, offer to do open houses for other agents (I'm sure they taught you this in training). Go look at the house you are holding open and then schedule previews of the other homes for sale in the immediate neighborhood.

As time permits, your priorities in previewing around an open house are as follows:

First, the competing listings - homes near your open house in the same general price range. It's also a good idea to preview any other homes for sale on the same block, regardless of price.

Second, any lower priced listings - homes near your open house that are priced lower than your open house.

Third, any higher priced listings - homes near your open house that are priced higher than your open house.

Fourth, some competing listings in comparable neighborhoods - similarly priced homes in other neighborhoods that are similar in appeal to the neighborhood of your open house.

I call this "Opinionated Previewing" because it's much easier to evaluate and absorb the appeal and features of a home if you have something to compare it to. Pretend you are working with a buyer who is looking for something similar to the home you are holding open (if all goes well at your open house, you may be!). At each home, ask yourself if this is a home you would show a prospective buyer. Look with a critical eye - does it show well? Does it seem to be priced appropriately? If it needs work, is there room in the market for an investor to make a little money? Does the home "wow" you when you walk in the door? Determine which ten listings are the best available and bring detailed printouts of these listings to the open house with you.

Have I lost you? Are you asking yourself, what's the point of all this previewing? Wasn't this chapter supposed to be about prospecting, not preparing for your open house?

Yes, and let me get back to topic. Every single time you preview with a purpose, I can almost guarantee you a sale or a listing. It's that powerful. I can't tell you how many times I previewed homes for one reason or another and that very night met someone who lived in the same building as a condo I looked at, or next door to a home I toured. Do you think you sound like a brand new agent when you can casually say to someone you just met, "Oh, there's a unit in your building for sale, isn't there? What a great location, right across from the park! What's going on with the construction next door?" You don't have to tell them you were out previewing *just that day*. No! You act as if you know every property in town because, after all, you are a professional real estate agent who keeps up on the market. Talk about building credibility! Real estate is almost always a hot topic in a social setting and if you sound as if you know your stuff, you'll hand out lots of business cards.

The trick is sounding as if you are the local expert. There's always someone in a roomful of people who is thinking about moving or buying an investment property, and the more you know about the market, the easier it is to catch his or her attention. When you speak with confidence about the real estate market, people listen.

Sure, when you're a rookie, you don't know the nuances of every neighborhood, condominium project or new subdivision. This will come with time. But the more you're out there, the quicker you'll be the expert. And it's great fun to be a Jim Peterson!

2. Capitalize on the Refinance Frenzy

A great way to build your market knowledge, practice pricing homes under pressure and market yourself to your SOI is to offer free competitive market analyses (CMA's) to your home-owning friends. Most homeowners frequently think about taking out a home equity loan, especially if interest rates have recently come down. But they need to have a certain amount of equity in the home to make the home equity loan worthwhile or even possible. That's where you come in.

Offer to do a quickie CMA to give them an idea of the current market value of their home. Go see the house

CMA

CMA stands for Competitive Market Analysis or Comparative Market Analysis. A CMA is a report prepared by a real estate agent to determine the market value of a home.

(at their convenience), preview the other active listings in the neighborhood, review the recent sales. Really do your homework; this is a great opportunity to impress someone who could be a referral source for you. Working through the intricacies of pricing a home is terrific practice too. And of course, you will then be familiar with yet another neighborhood, which will put you one step closer to being a Jim Peterson.

One caveat - well, two. You are not a licensed appraiser and your opinion of market value is meaningless to the bank or mortgage broker who will do the refinance for your friend. Be sure your friend knows that your CMA is only your opinion and that a licensed appraiser will likely come up with a different value, perhaps higher, perhaps lower.

Also, know that appraisers do not take into account currently active listings when appraising a home; they can only use data from sold homes. When you price a home for market, you definitely need to consider the competition, but an appraiser will not. So don't let your previewing push you to give your friend a higher estimate of market value if the sold data does not support that. Make sense?

Don't worry, Chapter Four gives you a complete lesson on preparing a market analysis and pricing a home.

If you do five of these CMA's, you will have taken a huge step toward being a professional real estate agent. The next time you only have 24 hours to prepare for a listing appointment, you'll be glad you got all this practice!

3. Go House-Hopping with a Friend

Do any of your friends own their home? Offer to take them on a tour of the homes for sale in their neighborhood, just for fun. If you're new and haven't yet worked with many (any?) buyers, you'll get practice selecting properties, setting showings, planning your route, opening lockboxes, and of course, showing houses. You'll also have a buddy to compare homes with and discuss the appeal and features of each. If you're showing homes in your friend's own neighborhood, he will be full of opinions for you!

Every First Year Agent Needs a Priscilla

Ah, the Priscillas of the world. Priscilla was the center of my world in my first year of real estate. Today, I might have fired Priscilla after a month or two, but in my first year, she was a gold mine - although of course I didn't appreciate her at the time.

About three months into my real estate career, my husband came home and announced he had a referral for me. His friend Priscilla mentioned to him that she was looking for a house and my dear husband was well-trained enough to tell her she ought to give me a call. And she did. I was so excited.

Priscilla didn't really know what she wanted, but she'd "know it when she saw it." Fair enough. She hated busy streets, but would scold me if I didn't tell her about a new listing on one of Denver's main thoroughfares. She turned up her nose at the west side of town, but would complain that I didn't show her that great Frank Lloyd Wright-style contemporary house in northwest Denver. Her requirements were three bedrooms and two bathrooms, but if I saw a one-bath house that had room for an additional bathroom, I shouldn't rule it out.

Oh, and Priscilla was always at least 45 minutes late.

Priscilla told me straight out that she was going to make lowball offers on homes, regardless of how well they were priced. Her philosophy was that the proof of a good negotiation is one where both parties feel a little uncomfortable with the outcome. This was during the real estate boom in Denver when there were multiple offers on any new listing that showed reasonably well. As a new agent, I didn't know any better and was just happy to have a warm body to put in my car.

I worked with Priscilla for nine months. During that period, we looked at more than ninety homes and wrote seven unaccepted offers. At one point I created a report for her demonstrating that all the homes we wrote offers on ended up selling at the asking price or even above. Not that it mattered to her - in her opinion, every home in Denver was "grossly overpriced."

So, why do I make the statement that "Every First Year Agent Needs a Priscilla"?

First, since Priscilla didn't know what she wanted, or where she wanted it, she got me into neighborhoods I didn't even know existed. Wonderful little enclaves that were off the beaten path, with charming names like Krisana Park, Arapahoe Acres, Aberdeen Village. I can't tell you how many times throughout my career my familiarity with these neighborhoods got me business. Priscilla essentially took me on a guided tour of Denver's hidden neighborhoods, thus enormously increasing my knowledge base and therefore my credibility. Exceptional market knowledge is by far the easiest way to prospect and build your business.

Here's an example of what I mean. One day I was doing an open house at an 1890 four-square home in central Denver. A youngish couple came in and started asking me questions about the home. I, fresh from open house training and in full rapport-building mode, asked them where they lived. They answered, with a naughty little smirk, "Aberdeen Village." I'm sure they got a kick out of messing with the real estate agents they met at open houses since Aberdeen Village is a little known enclave on the south side of town. That couple must have had fun watching agents struggle to look professional and knowledgeable when they didn't have a clue where Aberdeen Village was.

Well, Priscilla and I had just looked at a house in Aberdeen Village a few weeks earlier, so I was able to casually toss off, "Oh, Aberdeen Village - that's the neighborhood right off the lake with all the funky 60's houses, right?" They were impressed with this rookie agent! And, ended up hiring me to sell their Aberdeen Village home and represent them on the purchase of their next home. Ka-ching! $13,720 in commissions!

Priscilla kept me busy. In your first year or two of real estate, you probably aren't overloaded with business. You probably have days where you feel unproductive and, frankly, scared. The Priscillas of the world will teach you how to write contracts (you'll get lots of practice!), how to get around town, how to present a low offer - and, hopefully, you will eventually be paid for the education.

Did Priscilla ever buy a home? Yes, she did. One I found for her, a fabulous Santa Fe style-home on a park - it was worth waiting for. Funny, I have not really pursued repeat business from Priscilla, and wouldn't you know it - she won't lose my number. I still hear from her once a year or so when she gets restless and wants to move. So far, she hasn't. But if she does finally get serious, can I give her your number? Really, it will be good for you...

A Few More Things to Be Doing Right Now...
Start Building Your Team

During your first year, you must begin to develop your team. When I talk about Your Team, I am not referring to your assistant or your buyer agent. As a first-year real estate agent, you won't need those quite yet. I mean the outside contractors in your life who love you (because you give them business and make sure they get paid promptly) and will make your life as a real estate agent infinitely easier - they'll save your ass and your commission check and make you look goooood. You'll provide exceptional service, dramatically increase your closing ratio (i.e., reduce the number of sales that crash) and sleep much better at night. Once you have your team in place, you'll wonder how anyone practices real estate without one.

Here are the players:

HANDYMAN Every real estate agent must have a good handyman on call. Every real estate agent must have a good handyman on call. Every real estate agent must have a good handyman on call. He will save your commission over and over again. Find him, treat him well, pay him immediately. Be his top priority when you call on him. How agents operate without a great handyman is beyond me. A good handyman can handle plumbing and electrical repairs, carpentry, painting (although many choose not to paint) and garage door remote programming.

Bob is my handyman. He's personable, presentable and reasonable. He'll drive across town to fix an overflowing toilet and charge $20. He can fix anything and my clients adore him. I once had a plumbing issue with a 100-year-old clawfoot tub that three plumbers told me couldn't be fixed. Bob stewed over the problem for an hour or so and came up with a solution for about $70. If you can find a Bob in your town, he is like gold to you and your business. Don't let him get away.

HOUSE CLEANER   You can survive without a house cleaner, but I don't recommend it. You need someone reliable who is available on relatively short notice. Again, find her, treat her well, pay her immediately. More than once I found myself cleaning a home on the day of closing because the seller didn't do it. Or was sent a cleaning bill because my listing was "filthy" at the time of possession and the buyer had to hire Maids-R-Us, at $60/hour.

HVAC CONTRACTOR   You must have a good, reliable, reasonably priced heating and air conditioning contractor on your team. In Colorado, heating system concerns are among the biggest reasons real estate transactions fall apart at inspection. Ideally, find a one-man operation that needs your business, rather than a big company that does radio advertising. My independent HVAC contractor has replaced 100-year-old cast iron octopus-style furnaces for as little as $2,500, when others charge as much as $9,000. Heating contractors can usually help you out with plumbing issues too, leading me to my next category...

PLUMBER AND ELECTRICIAN   Depending on the expectations in your market, you may not use the services of a licensed plumber or electrician as often as you think you might. A good handyman can handle most of the plumbing and electrical work you'll run into. The nice thing about having a handyman do your work for you (besides his lower rates!) is that he can clean up any mess that he makes while doing the repair - for example, if he has to open up a wall to fix a leaking pipe, he can put the wall back together and paint it. Most licensed specialty contractors don't do that - they leave it for the homeowner to deal with.

The only times I ever hire a plumber or electrician is if a buyer or seller insists on having a licensed contractor make a repair at inspection or if a repair item requires a city permit that can only be pulled by a licensed plumber or electrician.

ROOFER Roof replacement prices vary widely and in most towns there will be a few roofers who cater to the real estate community. They are ready, willing and able to inspect a roof (hopefully at no cost) on a moment's notice and provide an estimate of repair or replacement in a timely manner. They know that more business will be forthcoming if they do a good job for you, so ask around your office to see if there are, indeed, a few "real estate agent roofers" in town.

STRUCTURAL ENGINEER AND STRUCTURAL CONTRACTOR If you live in a town where you will run into structural issues with the homes you sell, you'll need to have the names of both a structural engineer and a structural contractor. There's a huge difference between the two. A structural engineer evaluates a home and provides technical recommendations to correct structural deficiencies. The engineer does not make repairs and therefore generally has no idea of the cost of his or her recommendations. A structural contractor, on the other hand, is the person who actually makes structural repairs and can provide recommendations, as well as cost estimates.

Personally, I dislike the structural engineering racket. Most engineers are dour old codgers who hate older homes and love to kill perfectly good real estate deals. These guys scare buyers to death with predictions of gloom and doom if they don't make the recommended repairs right away and, since the buyers don't know how much repairs cost, they assume the worst. Whenever possible, I try to get my structural contractor in first. He tends to be surprisingly calming and his repair estimates are almost always far lower than the guesstimate provided by the structural engineer.

Other contractors to have on file are: a staging professional, a house painter and a hardwood floor installer/refinisher.

WHERE DO I FIND MY TEAM?

You aren't going to find them in the phone book. The team members you are looking for can't afford a big splashy yellow page ad. The best way to find reliable contractor-types is by keeping your antennae up. Look at bulletin boards in grocery stores, classified ads in the newspapers under "services," and if you have any builder friends, ask them who they use. If you are on the buyer side of a real estate transaction, notice who the listing agent used for any negotiated repairs. Once you have found one good contractor, ask him - he'll likely have friends in the other trades who would love to have your business. It's trial and error, but you will find them. And you will wonder how you ever closed a sale without them.

Here are a few more members for your team:

MORTGAGE BROKERS You'll need two or three good mortgage brokers. If you've worked with a mortgage broker in the past on personal home purchases (and were satisfied), by all means call him (or her). Ask your friends, your associates. What makes a mortgage broker "good"? Responsiveness! And creativity, the willingness to work with less-than-cherry borrowers, someone who is a good fit for your personality. None of which you'll know up front; you'll just have to test drive them. The good news is that there are mortgage brokers on every corner, and they'll be thrilled to get your business.

OTHER REAL ESTATE AGENTS Yes, other real estate agents can be valuable members of your team. Think referral fees. Free money! I choose not to work with foreclosures, short sales, commercial property, vacant land or rent-to-own buyers. But believe me, I have great resources in the real estate community for these types of transactions. Twenty to twenty-five percent commission for making a phone call? Sounds good to me.

Don't spend a lot of time searching for real estate agents to refer to - they will cross your path during the course of doing business. Make friends with them and keep their contact information current.

HOME INSPECTORS Oh, to have three great inspectors on my referral list! Right now I have one. If he's not available, my backups will do, but I'm just not as confident. I have gone through dozens of inspectors and found most of them less than satisfactory. Either they're classic deal-breakers (every house is a money pit) or, at the opposite extreme, they're in and out in under an hour. Finding good home inspectors is an ongoing challenge. Get referrals from other agents and your broker.

Continuing Education

Your first year is a good time to start acquiring designations. You have the time to spend in class (at least more than you'll have in years two to five), you'll hopefully learn something and at the end you'll have a fancy symbol to add to your business card.

The GRI (Graduate Realtor® Institute) and the ABR® (Accredited Buyer Representative) are two good programs for residential agents. The classes are not too expensive and most metropolitan areas offer the programs year round. I strongly recommend attending the classes rather than taking them online. I promise you will learn a lot and come away with some great ideas. It's also interesting to hear the chatter of other real estate agents, although at times you'll want to pull your hair out at some of the stupid, irrelevant questions and un-soulful commentary.

Many real estate boards offer ongoing continuing education classes on a variety of interesting topics. Classes on HUD homes and foreclosures could open new avenues of business for you or, conversely, convince you (as they did for me) that you don't want to mess with them. Take a class on 1031 Exchanges. You don't need to be an expert, but you need to know what they are.

Ethics and agency classes are always fun - if you like hearing how all your Standard Operating Procedures are illegal and/or unethical. You can always recognize a student fresh from an agency class - they have a dazed look on their face caused by the realization that they're just an audit or complaint away from professional disgrace. A Legal Issues class will do this for you too.

Consider a Contact Management Program

Earlier, I advised you to create your SOI using any program or system that you are comfortable with. I didn't want you getting bogged down or frustrated trying to learn a complicated program at this stage of your fledgling career.

But that doesn't mean you won't ever need one. While your Low Tech PDA (index cards) will get you started, it's no substitute for a great contact and contract management program, especially once you have listings, pending sales and buyers under contract.

I am fanatical about Top Producer. I absolutely could not run my business without it. It is probably far more powerful than I even know, but the three or four features I use are invaluable to me. I'm sure you can find other programs out there and feel free to shop around.

I use Top Producer for two main purposes. First, to track and maintain my SOI. All my contacts are entered into the system with as much information about them as I have. Name, address, phone, e-mail and birthday, of course, along with information about other properties they own and any contact notes I make. Pretty basic stuff.

I also track my web leads (leads generated by my online marketing) and expired listings (when I'm in the mood to prospect to them, not often!). The system reminds me to send birthday cards, and I've created a plan for anniversary cards to be sent out at intervals (one month, six months, one year, etc.) after the closing of a listing or buyer purchase.

However, the more important use I have for my beloved Top Producer is contract management. All my active listings, buyers under contract and listings under contract are entered into the system with a comprehensive follow-up program I created from my checklists. These checklists are described later in the book and can be input directly into your Top Producer if you like. Every day I check my To-Do list online and nothing ever slips through the cracks. As long as it's on my list...

When you only have a few deals going on, this may seem more complicated than it's worth. But when (not if) your business takes off, you won't have time to figure out the program, so practice now! At one point in my career, my partner and I had 40 listings and 20 pending sales and I never broke a sweat keeping track of dates, deadlines and duties.

I also use Top Producer to track personal dates, such as reminders regarding my rental properties (shut down the sprinkler system in October, change the furnace filters every month, etc.), reminders to give my dogs their heartworm pills, even reminders to pay my bills when I get really busy.

* * *

My boyfriend's 13-year-old daughter, Elizabeth, made me a birthday cake, in my kitchen. I was banished to my bedroom so that she could surprise me. Good time for a nap, I figured! But every few minutes, Elizabeth came knocking at my door asking questions like, "Where do you keep the vanilla?" "What's the difference between olive oil and canola oil?" "Where do you keep the mixer?" I could feel her frustration building - I'm sure it had sounded like such a good idea at the time - but it was harder than she thought it would be.

This is how you will feel setting up your first showings or putting together your first listing presentation. Like a 13-year old in unfamiliar surroundings (her father's girlfriend's kitchen or you staring at your computer), doing something new for the first time (baking a cake or writing your first offer), you'll be unpleasantly surprised, even panicked, by how much you don't know.

But Elizabeth persevered and finished the cake. You will too, and it won't be long before setting showings and preparing for listing presentations will be second nature to you. To help get you there quicker, looking like a pro all the way - read on!

> ### JENNIFER'S $0.02...
>
> *Don't be afraid to tell mortgage brokers, title representatives, inspectors or appraisers that you're new. Even the agent on the other end of the deal, if he seems at all soulful. Most experienced real estate agents will treat you far better if you admit to your inexperience rather than bluff your way through. It's crystal clear to me when I'm dealing with a rookie, and when they get cocky and arrogant, I can't help being a little testy myself. Especially when they're dead wrong about something. If an agent tells me up front that he or she is new, I'll go out of my way to make their experience pleasant.*

3

Working with Buyers
Helping them find "The One"

As a new real estate agent, it's likely you'll work with more buyers than sellers early on. Your broker will walk you through the showing protocol of your market area - scheduling showings, showing appointment windows, lockbox and/or key pickup. This part is real easy. My job here is to help you with the nuances that they don't teach you in real estate school or office training, and give you some hints so you look as if you've been showing houses to buyers for years!

THE HOME-BUYING PROCESS

Although each market has its nuances, the overall process of working with buyers looks something like this:

1. Pre-qualify the buyer

2. Show properties to the buyer

3. Find "The One" and make a written offer on it

4. Negotiate the offer with the seller's agent

5. If the offer is successfully negotiated, start scheduling inspections

6. Buyer obtains loan approval

7. Final Walk-thru

8. Closing

We'll examine each step in detail.

Pre-Qualifying Buyers

Many real estate instructors make quite a fuss about financially pre-qualifying your buyers. They advise you to either pre-qualify them yourself (I've never done this) or send them off to your lender right away. I more or less agree. However, remember to treat your new buyer the way you would like

> **LENDER**
> *The person who handles the buyer's loan, also known as a mortgage broker.*

to be treated. Imagine how you would feel if, at your first meeting with a real estate agent, he only seemed to care about your financial qualifications and not about your housing needs. When you are working with a brand new buyer, you need to build rapport if you ever want to hear from him or her again. If you immediately shuttle him off to your lender as if you couldn't be bothered even talking with him, you will likely lose that buyer to another, more soulful agent who makes him feel special.

Besides, it won't hurt you to "waste" your time talking with a buyer who isn't qualified to purchase a home just yet. It won't even hurt you to show her homes once or twice; if nothing else, you'll add a little something to your market knowledge - always a good thing. If she can't buy a

> **CAUTION!**
> *Beware of writing an offer for a buyer who hasn't yet spoken with a lender; it's not only a waste of time, it's disrespectful to the seller, the listing agent and the entire process.*

house today, she may very well be able to buy in a year (and that year will be here before you know it).

But there's a difference between someone who isn't quite ready to buy and someone who is just using you to entertain her. It's perfectly reasonable for you to ask a new buyer prospect to call a lender so both of you have a solid price range to work with. If the buyer resists you at this point, you can safely assume she isn't serious and will likely vanish on you. A buyer who wants to buy a house is looking to you for guidance on the process. If you tell a real buyer to call a lender, she will happily call a lender.

Showing Houses to Buyers

It looks and sounds a lot easier than it is. I still struggle sometimes picking the right homes to show buyers, especially if I'm working in an unfamiliar neighborhood. If you live in a metropolitan area, it will be years before you know your way around every neighborhood in town, if ever. It's mortifying to get lost while showing houses, and if your buyer is from out of town - in town for the weekend to buy a house - you might even lose her business if you don't appear to know your city.

Please see "Fine-Tuning Your Buyer Skills - Selecting Homes to Show Your Buyer" later in this chapter for more tips on showing property.

The Buyer Showing Packet

I give my buyer detailed printouts of all the listings we are looking at, in the order of appearance. That's it. Nothing fancy, just easy to assemble and revise at the last minute. Believe me, it's more than many agents do for their buyers.

Find the One, Make an Offer

You will develop your own style for showing homes and I don't think there's one "right" way to do it. Some agents follow their buyers around, pointing out the obvious. "And this is the kitchen!" I let my buyers wander around as they please while I explore the house on my own. It allows them to discover the home for themselves without distracting input from me.

You will also develop a knack for recognizing when buyers want to make an offer on a house - when to push them, when to back off. Many real estate books will give you a variety of closing methods designed to get your buyer to the table writing an offer. I tend toward the soft sell, perhaps even softer than I should, because buyers do need to be pushed a little sometimes. They want to buy, but are scared. Or perhaps they are waiting for you to show them what the next step is (it's obvious to you, but not to them).

Your personality and personal style will lead you down the correct path, for you. But at the very least, offer to draft up a contract *for their review*.

If your buyers think they have found a house they love, but aren't sure, tread carefully. I think the old cliche' is true - that they will know it when they see it, and I tell my buyers this. I don't want them to make an offer on a home they don't love because they will probably want out of the deal somewhere down the road. Lots of hassle for me, an inconvenience to the sellers and a real buzz-kill for the buyers. If I sense that my buyers are ambivalent about a home, even if they're ready to make an offer, I'll try to put them off overnight. I don't want them to feel undue pressure from me because it will be All My Fault when they can't sleep a few nights later, wracked with buyer's remorse.

Some buyers simply aren't emotional, but this is the exception, not the norm. Even professional investors get a little excited when you find them a good deal. Buyers who aren't excited are either worried about something they haven't told you about or aren't emotionally attached to the home. Assure them that they have all the time in the world (as far as you're concerned) and that it may take several trips to find the right house. When they see that you're not pressuring them to make a quick decision, their trust in you will increase dramatically, making your job easier and much more fun.

Another pitfall to watch for is if a buyer falls head over heels in love with a house that you suspect isn't big enough for him. When he starts talking about building an addition or selling his grandmother's furniture because it won't fit in the tiny living room, you know he's getting carried away emotionally. In the light of (another) day, he may realize that this home simply won't work for him. If he insists on making an offer right away, you can't fight him and don't try. He is an adult, after all, and will resent you trying to tell him what to do. The best you can do is advise him to think about it overnight to make sure the size of the home is something he will be happy with.

Preparing the Offer

Explain to your buyer that the offer is a written proposal between the buyer and the seller. The offer outlines the buyer's desired price, financial terms, dates and deadlines, personal property inclusions, etc. If the seller signs the offer as written, the offer becomes a binding contract. If the seller makes any changes to the offer, in the form of a counterproposal, the seller has technically rejected the offer and the buyer is free to walk away. In most states, either party is free to rescind his offer or counteroffer at any time prior to written acceptance by the other party. *(Please check with your broker for any local variances.)*

Spend at least an hour going through the purchase contract with your buyer. Explain in detail how the inspection provision works since this is an area of significant concern for buyers. Also ensure that your buyer understands her rights and responsibilities regarding the loan application and approval process. You'll develop your own "rap" for explaining contracts to buyers, but try to keep in mind that this may be the first time your buyer has ever seen a real estate purchase contract. She may be making assumptions she doesn't know to ask you about. For example, make sure she knows that her earnest money deposit check will be cashed if the offer is accepted. I've found that many buyers think it is held until closing.

EARNEST MONEY

The deposit check written by the buyer when making an offer on a property. If the offer is successfully negotiated, earnest money is deposited into an escrow account and credited back to the buyer at closing. If the buyer defaults on the contract, the earnest money may be retained by the seller.

BUYER AGENT

The real estate agent representing the buyer, usually with a written buyer agency agreement.

The purchase contract is overwhelming and intimidating. Assure your buyer that you will be carefully tracking the deadlines with her, so she need not worry about missing an important date. Later in this chapter, we'll discuss date tracking in more detail.

EVERYONE LIKES TO NEGOTIATE...

...regardless of any claim to the contrary. It's tempting to put together a low offer for a buyer and declare to the listing agent that, "This is our final and best offer." But it won't work. The seller doesn't want to accept an offer as written, unless it's full price, and a buyer will actually be dismayed if her first (low) offer is accepted. She'll wonder if she could have/should have offered less.

As a buyer agent, encourage strong offers, but remember that you represent your buyer, not your commission check. If your buyer wants to offer low, even after you've shown her data that indicates the home is priced fairly, go ahead and put the offer together. Don't whine and fuss and by all means, don't be embarrassed about presenting the offer to the listing agent. Your job is to get your buyer client the best price and if your words or body language indicate to the listing agent that your offer sucks and you know it - you just breached your duty to your buyer.

Besides, you never know what the seller will accept. I've tried to convince my buyers to offer more than they want to (and I usually lose) and lo and behold - the seller accepts their low offer! Talk about losing credibility with my buyers in a single bound. Oops. I'm making light of the situation, but it can get pretty ugly, pretty quickly. If you give your buyer any reason to suspect that you don't have his best interest at heart, you will lose his trust and probably his business.

That said, you can make the choice to let your buyer go if he truly is not motivated. If a buyer is motivated, he will usually abandon the lowball-offer strategy after trying it a few times.

I encourage buyers to attempt to meet the seller's needs on any items that aren't that important to the buyer. If price is the buyer's hot button (and it almost always is), try to accommodate the seller's desired closing date. If the buyer needs to extend the closing date beyond the norm, or has a house to sell, make the offer price a little more appealing. Your negotiating skills and instincts will improve with each offer you write.

Let's assume you've successfully negotiated your offer and you're now under contract! Yippeeeeeeee!

Start Scheduling Inspections

Don't spend your commission check quite yet. In some markets, inspections can kill a significant number of your sales if you're having a run of bad luck.

The topic of inspections is so important that I have devoted an entire chapter to it. Don't sell any homes until you read Chapter Six!

The Final Stretch - Moving Toward Closing

Okay, if you're through inspection, it's safe to breathe a sigh of relief. The inspection is often the toughest part of a residential home sale. Now the experts take over. That would be the mortgage broker, the title company and the appraiser. Your job at this point is to ensure that the inspection items are completed as agreed, that the closing is scheduled and that the loan is progressing smoothly.

INSPECTION

This is the contractually agreed-upon time period where the buyer has the right to inspect the physical condition of the property. In some regions, this could include an investigation into the crime rates, public school data, demographics or any other non-physical "feature" of the property. If the buyer is dissatisfied with the condition of the property, physical or otherwise, he must object before the inspection objection deadline or the seller can assume that the buyer accepts the property "as is."

TITLE COMPANY

The company that provides title insurance and closing services. The title company handles collection and distribution of funds, conducts the closing and ensures clear title to the buyer.

Buyer Gets Loan Approval

The final contingency is usually loan approval. Assuming the buyer's lender is competent, this should require no more than a few phone calls to the lender to ensure that the loan is on track. Be sure to call the lender on the day before the formal loan approval deadline to see if an extension will be needed, so you can prepare to grovel before the listing agent.

FINAL WALK-THRU

Schedule your final walk-thru with your buyer and the listing agent. The purpose of the walk-thru is to confirm that inspection items have been completed (take your inspection paperwork!), that the sellers appear to be moving out and that the home is in the same condition as it was at inspection, "normal wear and tear excepted."

> **CAUTION!**
> *Be sure to call the listing agent before your walk-thru to confirm that all inspection items are complete; your buyer will be understandably concerned, and you will look clueless and even incompetent if you are surprised by items left undone.*

CLOSING

Closing protocol is different across the country. In some markets, the buyers and sellers all get together in one room and have a little key exchange party, facilitated by the title company. In others, the buyers and sellers never even meet. In resort markets, it is common that no one attends the closing - all paperwork is done through the mail.

Your responsibilities for the closing are to review the closing statement for accuracy, communicate to your buyer the amount and type of funds (cashier's check, wire transfer, etc.) needed to close, ensure that you have the required signatures on all contracts and disclosures, arrange the key exchange for your buyer and make sure the buyer has documentation for all inspection items requiring proof.

Oh, yes - and collect your commission check! Woo hoo!

CLOSING GIFTS

For years I spent hours coming up with the perfect gift for each of my wonderful clients. It was probably one of the biggest time and money wasters in my business. First, closings are a hectic time for buyers and sellers. They are in the process of uprooting their lives and they have a lot on their minds. Sure, your closing gift is nice, but it's just not going to get the attention it deserves at this particular time. It might just be one more thing they have to pack and move.

A much better idea is to contact the client a month or so later and make arrangements to drop off a gift, if you must. Because initiating social encounters is intimidating for me, just calling a client to say hi does not come naturally. Having an excuse to call (i.e., to drop off my fabulous closing gift) makes it much easier for me. If "warm"-calling comes naturally for you, you really don't need the gift.

Checklist For Buyers-Under-Contract

Here is the first of several checklists for you! This checklist addresses the items that are your responsibility during the period from contract to closing, as the buyer agent. A simpler version of the checklist without my commentary is available in the Appendix and on my website (www.sellwithsoul.com). It is formatted to be used as a check-off sheet for each buyer if you aren't yet using a contract management program.

IMMEDIATELY AFTER CONTRACT IS EXECUTED

√   Put contract dates in your contract manager program
Important dates include any objection deadlines (inspection, insurance, title, covenant review, appraisal, etc.), loan approval or any other agreements made in the contract. If you don't use a contract management program, enter these dates in your planner.

√   Fax the executed contract and copy of earnest money to the buyer's lender

√   Deliver the property disclosures to your buyer and get signatures

√   Deliver earnest money check to listing agent, if not already done

√   Give the buyer the HOA contact and questionnaire
Do so if applicable. See Chapter Eight for more information on the questionnaire.

√   Advise the buyer to schedule the inspection(s)

FIRST WEEK AFTER CONTRACT EXECUTION

√ Call the buyer's lender to confirm loan application

√ Ask buyer's lender to delay appraisal until after the inspection period

If the appraisal is ordered too soon, a chance exists that the appraiser will complete the appraisal before the inspection is successfully negotiated. If the buyer terminates the contract due to inspection issues, he could still be charged for the appraisal. I always try to head this off with the lender.

√ Deliver signed property disclosures to listing agent

√ Advise the buyer to look into hazard insurance

√ Call buyer's lender to check in

√ Schedule the closing (after inspection is resolved)

10 DAYS TO ONE WEEK PRIOR TO CLOSING

√ Arrange Power of Attorney or mail-out close, if applicable

If your buyer will not attend closing, make sure the title company and lender are aware of this way ahead of time. Either the buyer will need to designate someone to sign for him (and it shouldn't be you), or the entire package will be mailed or e-mailed to him. Typically, the title company will coordinate this for you, as long as they know about it.

√ Confirm that the inspection items are complete - ask for documentation

√ Schedule the walk-thru

√ Are there any changes that need to be communicated to the lender or title company?

Many times, contract provisions will be changed or negotiated and no one remembers to let the lender and/or title company know. If material changes are a surprise to the lender or title company, you may not have a closing when you planned!

√   Remind the buyer to call utility companies to transfer service (provide phone numbers)

1-2 DAYS BEFORE CLOSING

√   Confirm with all parties the closing date, time and place

√   Review the closing statement
At least half the time the closing statement will have an error or two. Review it closely. Don't forget any negotiated credits for closing costs or inspection items. Ensure that the earnest money has been credited. If you haven't yet received a closing statement from the lender or title company, call to find out why.

√   Call the buyer with closing figures
After you have blessed the closing figures, call your buyer to let her know how much money she needs to bring to the closing. Make sure she knows that her funds need to be in the form of a cashiers check, not a personal check! Remind her to bring identification.

√   Prepare the file for closing
Ensure that all documents and disclosures are signed. Review the contract and any amendments to refresh your memory on items to be confirmed prior to closing. Make sure the file is organized so that you will be able to quickly answer any questions that may arise at closing. If your office provides a list of required documents that you must turn in after closing (to get your paycheck), review the checklist and take it with you.

AFTER CLOSING

√   Turn in the closed file to the office manager...so you get paid!

√   Update your buyer's address in your SOI manager

√   Add buyer to your post-closing follow-up plan
I have a follow-up plan that reminds me to send greeting cards to my clients at intervals after closing. I send a card one month, six months, one year, two years and three years after closing. I don't necessarily send "Happy Six Month" anniversary cards, just something to let them know

I still exist and am still in real estate. Sometimes I'll send a little gift, like a $10 Starbucks gift card, just thanking them again for their business.

√ Call buyer a few days after move-in
Don't be accused of getting your commission check and disappearing off the face of the earth. This is definitely Old School behavior! Usually the buyer is thrilled with her new home, but if a problem has arisen, this is a golden opportunity for you to help. It may be contrary to your natural instincts to go looking for trouble, but the bonus points you'll rack up are worth the extra hassle.

I once worked with a first-time buyer who was so nervous about buying a home that he literally got the flu right before closing. The thought of being a homeowner with homeowner responsibilities was just about more than he could handle. He did close however and I breathed a sigh of relief. When I called him a few days after closing to check in, he said that the outlet for the dryer didn't work and he was in a panic. He asked me if I would call the previous owner and get him to fix it. I was all set to explain to him that once he closed on the house, these sorts of problems would come up and he'd have to deal with them. Luckily, my more soulful instincts kicked in and I stopped myself. I called the previous owner and amazingly, he sent over his handyman right away to fix the plug. Problem solved. Don't be afraid of reasonable requests - every once in a while you'll be pleasantly surprised and maybe even look like a hero. Especially to those nervous first-time buyers.

Fine-Tuning Your Buyer Skills
Buyer Agency ~ Sign 'Em up Before You Put 'Em in Your Car!?

This is the battle cry of many new and experienced buyer agents. I'm referring to "buyer agency," a legal, contractual relationship between a real estate agent and his buyer client.

Our handling of buyer agency is one of my pet peeves about the real estate industry. Not to be confused with a required agency disclosure, a buyer agency agreement obligates the buyer to the agent for a specified period of time. If the buyer purchases a home during the contract period, the buyer is contractually agreeing to ensure that his agent gets a commission on that home. Once a buyer signs a buyer agency agreement, he is bound to that agent. If he purchases a home using another agent, he may be obligated to pay both agents a commission.

To be fair, most buyer agency agreements create many more obligations from the agent to the buyer; in fact, if truly understood, the contract is typically more onerous on the agent than on the buyer. If you don't believe me, go review the buyer agency contract again. When presented at the appropriate time, I don't have too many objections to the contract. However, I think it is obnoxious and disrespectful to ask someone you just met to commit to you before she knows much about you. She has no idea if you return your phone calls promptly - if you even know much about this buyer's preferred neighborhoods - or if the two of you will have enough rapport to survive the stresses of buying a home.

I think our pushing of buyer agency is one of the reasons the public doesn't respect real estate agents. And, to hear many agents talk, this disrespect is warranted. Have you heard anyone in your office say "I got 'em signed up" or "I won't put a buyer in my car without a signed buyer agency"? Seems to me that we ought to be proving ourselves to our prospects before asking for a commitment.

If it weren't required by law, I wouldn't do buyer agency agreements at all. I see a broker/buyer relationship as just that, a relationship. Sort of like marriage - a signed piece of paper may not keep two people together if the relationship is not satisfying to both parties. If I prove myself to a buyer, he's going to stick with me. If I don't, he should be allowed to look elsewhere for real estate assistance. If your intent is to force a buyer to stay with you, do it by making yourself indispensable, not by pushing a piece of paper at him. Sure, there are the random situations where your buyer accidentally buys a home from a builder or an agent sitting at an open house, but that's your fault! Have the conversation with your buyers about how you get paid - and why they should bring you in on any and all negotiations.

It will happen - you'll get a call from the buyer whom you've chauffeured all over town and taken to lunch telling you that she found the perfect FSBO and made an offer without you. If you can get your foot in the door at this point, go for it. If not, move on. Please check with your soul on this before you go after the commission from the buyer, even if you have a buyer agency agreement in place - these things happen, learn from them and don't give your buyer any ammunition to blast your name with. You might even want to be gracious about it and offer a little help. You never know, there might be a future referral in it for you.

Selecting the Right Homes to Show Your Buyer

As mentioned earlier, selecting the right homes to show a buyer, especially a new buyer, is tougher than you might think. This is your one opportunity to make a great first impression - buyers subconsciously expect you to intuitively know what they're looking for, even if they don't. A great way to lose a new buyer is to show him homes he has absolutely no interest in. He may decide that you and he are not a good fit, or he may even lose his enthusiasm for buying a home at all. The next phone call you get is the one telling you he found a great rental house and signed a one-year lease.

So, you need to do your homework ahead of time, both with your new buyer and with the market. The first step, of course, is to find out what your buyer is looking for. A buyer's preferred neighborhood is probably the most important factor. If he is unfamiliar with your city, find out what kind of neighborhood he thinks he'd like - urban, suburban, rural, mountains, coastal? Any particular commuting distance? Does he like charming older homes near the city center or new contemporary homes near the shopping malls? Price range?

Next, move to your buyer's "must-have" list. Number of bedrooms, baths, garage? Any special needs? Don't get too specific though. Pushing buyers for too many details is counterproductive, believe it or not. If you keep pushing, he may start making things up to please you. Doesn't everyone want a garage and more than one bath? But he might not really care that much and, if you limit your search to his non-critical parameters, you'll miss a lot of great homes.

The other danger in asking for too many details is that your buyer will start telling you things like, "I really want a window over the kitchen sink" or "I want an open floor plan with lots of light." Depending on your inventory, you may end up with nothing to show her if you rely strictly on her wish list.

61

And if you show her homes that don't meet her "requirements," she may think you weren't listening. You (and she) need to gauge her reactions to different styles of homes in person. Remember, buyers don't shop for homes every day and don't really know what they will respond to until they've seen it.

I tell new buyers that our first trip out together is a fishing expedition. That we probably won't find a house for them to buy that first day. Our goal is to get them to start developing opinions on neighborhood, style, vintage and features, and to test their tolerance for fix-up. This subtly assures them that you are looking out for their best interests and that you won't push them to make a decision until they're darn good and ready. Don't worry, it won't slow down their home-buying decision process; if they find a house they like on the first trip out, they'll buy it regardless of what you told them ahead of time.

ARE BUYERS REALLY LIARS?

Buyers can be hard to nail down and you'll hear agents talk about the "Buyers Are Liars" phenomenon. It's a phrase usually used in frustration either when an agent loses a buyer or when he's at his wit's end showing homes that the buyer says work for her, but don't inspire her to make an offer. It simply means that buyers don't really know what they want, and often it's true.

When I was shopping for a second home in Alabama, I told my agent that my "must-have's" were four bedrooms, a two-car garage and high-speed Internet access. What did I buy? A three-bedroom home with no garage and dial-up access only. But my agent was sharp enough to switch gears in the middle of our search when she saw that I was emotionally responding to homes in the country, even if they didn't have everything I claimed I had to have.

To pick out the best homes to show on your first showing tour, go through your MLS and find around 20 homes that might work for this buyer, based on his location preferences and his "must-have" list. Unless you're absolutely sure that your buyer wants a fix-up home, narrow down your list to homes that appear to be in excellent condition. (See "Most Fix-Up Buyers Aren't," following this section.)

Then, go preview all of them. I promise you, you'll be glad you did. At least half of the homes you preview will have a fatal flaw (an unfixable "feature" of a home that makes it unappealing to the majority of buyers - e.g., proximity to a highway or an unusually small yard–making the home a bad investment). These are easily eliminated from your tour. You are looking for the best five-to-nine homes to show your buyer. In a strong seller's market, don't be surprised if you can't find enough good homes to show! If this is the case, either find a few more truly wonderful homes that don't quite meet your buyer's criteria, or go ahead and show a few homes that have all the buyer's requirements but don't show as well.

> **CAUTION!**
> *Beware of showing a home that backs to a highway or has some other major location flaw - it will appear to your buyer that you don't know your market or don't care about his home as an investment. If he picks out such a home from an Internet search or by driving around, then by all means show it to him, but don't pick it out yourself. Buyers assume we are familiar with every house in town, so when we show a house that is clearly a bad investment, a buyer will think we're stupid, uncaring or worse - inexperienced.*

I know the Denver market, especially the central neighborhoods. Yet I still usually preview before going out with a new buyer, although now that my MLS has interior photos for most listings, sometimes I'll skip this step. However, if I'm showing homes in the suburbs (definitely not my specialty), I always, always, always preview. At the very least, I drive by all the homes, one, to make sure the location is acceptable and two, to make sure I can find them!

This last is an important point. Nothing is more unraveling than getting lost with a buyer in your car. Talk about putting your antiperspirant to work. Denver proper is laid out in a grid and most streets are alphabetical (Ash, Birch, Cherry, Dexter), so getting around is a breeze. However, in the suburbs, you might find 67th Circle, 67th Drive, 67th Avenue, 67th Place - with lots of cul-de-sacs and dead ends. My first year I worked in the foothills west of Denver, which were a nightmare to navigate. Homes could be five tedious miles up winding, unmarked roads, some not even on my map. Previewing for buyers could take all day, but was worth every hairpin turn.

You might think condos would be easier - after all, once you find the complex, you know you're in the right place. Actually, I find condos to be more difficult to show and even more important to preview. First, in a large complex, just finding the unit can be a challenge and that's before you've hunted down the lockbox! Many condominiums and lofts are in secured buildings, so the lockbox is placed outside on the front railing. There might be 20 other lockboxes hanging there too! Or, I've seen units where the door handle design isn't conducive to hanging a lockbox, so the lockbox is hiding in a nearby stairwell. High-rise buildings might require you to check in with the front desk to pick up a key.

You'll be a basket-case after your day of showings if you aren't prepared. If you look the slightest bit flustered in front of your buyer, your credibility will take a huge hit and you might even lose the buyer. Have I made you nervous? I hope so, because it's far better to let your nervousness force you to prepare than to be cocky and make a fool of yourself.

Make like a Boy Scout - and Be Prepared!

Most Fix-Up Buyers Aren't

I'd guess that 70% of my new buyer clients identify themselves as potential "fix-up buyers." They enthusiastically support the idea of replacing carpet, painting walls, redoing a kitchen. They want some of that good old sweat equity in their pocket and it's trendy to say you want to fix up a property, especially during boom years when everyone seems to be doing it profitably.

Don't believe them. What buyers intellectually know and what they emotionally respond to are two very different things. In my experience fewer than 10% of my buyer clients were truly looking for a fix-up home.

So don't waste your time or damage your credibility. Unless your buyer is a contractor looking for a fix-n-flip, show only the nicest homes to your new buyer on your first trip out. Maybe throw in a dated (I said dated, not dumpy) home or two to test his tolerance, but otherwise, Pottery Barn homes only. Well-decorated, great street appeal, nice smelling - you get the point. The vast majority of buyers will not respond to grandma's house, regardless of what a great deal it is. They want to see Martha Stewart.

If you ignore this advice and show them homes they have no emotional response to, you will have irreparably damaged your credibility and taken their enthusiasm down a few notches. You might even lose the buyers after they stumble into a beautifully presented open house in their price range and wonder why you didn't show it to them. They will never remember telling you they wanted to "fix up" a home.

After your first showing date, if the buyer tells you he wants to look at homes that need more work, then by all means, comply with his wishes. But at first, you are much better off erring on the Pottery Barn side.

Let Your Buyer's Emotions Make the Decision, Not Yours

There is an interesting phenomenon in real estate sales that will give you fits until you recognize it. Here's a common scenario...

You are out previewing and you find The One for your difficult buyer. It's everything she ever wanted, at the right price, in the right neighborhood. You are so excited, you call her from the living room and gush over how you have finally found the house for her.

You insist she look at the home right away because you know it will sell quickly. You lead her in the door and - nothing. She is lukewarm. She may try to be polite because she sees how excited *you* are, but she finds fault with every room, the location, the yard—you are crushed and frustrated and consider firing her on the spot.

Or, a slight twist on the above. You are working with a couple. You and the wife usually preview the properties together so that you only show the best ones to her husband 'cause he's so busy. You and the missus find The One. She's euphoric, delirious, can't wait to show it to her husband. She's already moving in. You catch on to the excitement and you both call him from the house to tell him all about the wonderful home. You pass the cell phone back and forth between you, so you can share in the excitement of telling him all the details.

You show him the house as soon as he can get away from work. Thud. He doesn't like it at all. Even though it's everything he said he wanted, he just doesn't warm up to it. The wife and husband get into a terrible fight and decide not to buy a house at all. You're glad you're not going home with them, but you're incredibly discouraged at his reaction. "What a controlling jerk he is!" you say to yourself.

This happens all the time. The explanation is that buyers need to discover The One for themselves. It's human nature to resist being told what to do, and your strong reaction is essentially that - telling the buyers that they are going to buy this house.

Scenario #2 is caused primarily by jealousy. Yes, jealousy. The spouse who doesn't participate in the home search, even at his or her request (I'm not assuming that all husbands work and all wives shop for homes; I've seen it happen equally with both sexes) feels left out. He may feel that you are out having a good time with his wife while he's "stuck" at work. He may even worry that you and his wife are out flirting with men (if you're female), or flirting with each other (if you're male). These aren't rational reactions, but they're there - underneath the lackluster response to the dream home. It's his way of controlling the situation even though he agreed to take a back seat in the process. He may know darn good and well that his wife is going to make the final decision, but that doesn't mean he's 100% comfortable with it.

So, hopefully the solution to both scenarios is obvious. Control your emotions. In Scenario #1, calmly call your buyer and tell her you found an interesting home she should look at. Maybe come up with a few others to show at the same time. Don't rave about the home or pressure her to come see right away.

In Scenario #2, you have two ways (used in conjunction) to head off this problem. First, insist that the husband accompany you and his wife on your first outing. This way he feels involved in the process and you can see how he responds to homes. After one showing tour, he will feel more in control and that he is "handing off" house-hunting responsibilities to his wife instead of being shut out. Secondly, convince the wife to control her emotions when you do find a great house. She may not believe you when you explain how the husband might react to her excitement. If necessary, set up a few other homes to show him at the same time you show him The One. He needs to feel as if he had a choice and that his wife (and you) respect his opinion and his choice.

Another emotional decision that must be made by your buyer, not by you, is a comfort level with location. You may know that a neighborhood is in the process of "turning around" (although Fair Housing laws limit what you can say about this), and would make a great investment for your buyer. But if your buyer isn't as comfortable as you are, don't push! Give your opinion once and let him do his own research and soul searching. You will lose if your buyer gives in to your pressure and purchases a home against his gut instinct. If he (or his neighbors) are burglarized, which can happen anywhere, it will be All Your Fault. As a real estate agent, you may always be thinking "investment" (and you should be), but this is not the typical priority of a buyer, especially a first-time buyer.

I once helped some adorable first-time buyers who should have bought a home in the suburbs, but fancied themselves urban dwellers. Like many first-time buyers, they desired a neighborhood they couldn't afford. However, their favored neighborhood had more affordable housing on its fringes and they were willing to explore that option.

We found a great home in their price range. It was located in an up-and-coming neighborhood that offered almost guaranteed market appreciation as the neighborhood improved. I knew it was a great investment. They were clearly hesitant about the location, but unfortunately, I pushed and wouldn't take no for an answer. We put the home under contract and my buyers pretended to be excited. I overlooked their discomfort and moved forward with scheduling the inspection.

When we arrived for the home inspection, the tenant greeted us at the door with a detailed description of a robbery in the home the previous night. A man had broken through the back door, come into her bedroom and taken her jewelry along with some other items, before running out. The tenant was hysterical. My buyers were speechless. Thankfully, my good sense kicked in (better late than never) and, rather than try to convince them that this was probably an isolated event, I advised them to cancel the inspection right then. I assured them that we could easily terminate the contract under our inspection rights and resume our house hunt.

Which is what my buyers eventually did. I found them much less of a home in a much safer neighborhood and they are still happily living there.

Please keep in mind that your commission, regardless of how badly you need it, is secondary to your buyers' wants and needs. Your job is to represent and protect their interests, not yours. You will win far more brownie points by risking your commission (buyers aren't stupid, they know how you are paid, or at least they should) than you will trying to sell them on a property or situation they are clearly uncomfortable with. The minute a buyer feels that you are placing more importance on your paycheck than on his needs, you have lost his trust. In a buyer's mind, it is not market knowledge and contractual expertise that earns trust, it the feeling that you are truly on his side.

In fact, the more you "risk your paycheck" in front of your buyers, the more they will trust you. I had an investor client who told everyone about "Jennifer's nose wrinkle." Apparently I made a face whenever we walked into a home that I didn't think was a good buy for him. He told his friends that he knew right then that we might as well leave because Jennifer wasn't going to let him buy that house. It was meant as a sincere compliment and I took it as such. And, his friends all called me when they needed real estate service.

"Special" Buyers

There are two categories of buyers who deserve their own "special" discussion, because both can be gold mines for you - or make you dread getting up in the morning. I guarantee that you will have lots of fun "learning experiences" when you work with these special folks - investors and out-of-town buyers.

Investors

New agents tend to get a lot of amateur investors to work with. Amateur investors are relatively handy people who have a little cash and some spare time on their hands and have heard rumors of quick-n-easy money to be made renovating beautiful old Victorian homes. During the real estate boom in Denver, I worked almost exclusively with investors, which was profitable yet brain damaging and just plain hard work.

One good investor client can make your year, or at least give you a great head start. A bad one will make you wish you had chosen a different profession. You'll learn the difference, but remember - in your first year or two of real estate, everything is a learning experience and there is value in every experience you have, whether or not it results in a paycheck.

So, first, what is a "good" investor?

A good investor takes the process seriously. When you call your investor with a hot property, he wants to look at it right away. He shows up with his laptop computer, ready to input cost estimates into his prepared spreadsheet. If the numbers look as if they might work, he wants to make an offer right away - not tomorrow, not next week after he's gotten bids from three different contractors. He's reasonable with his offer - sure, he might lowball, but he is sensitive to the needs of the seller too. He'll try to make his offer as attractive as possible with regard to closing dates, inspection conditions and loan approvals.

If your offer is successfully negotiated, he'll get his inspections done quickly and won't get fussy over the minor issues. He understands that a home that is a good cosmetic fix-up project will probably have other maintenance issues too.

A good investor is well-qualified financially. He's not going to try to do an FHA or low down-payment loan that will get kicked back at the appraisal due to the poor condition of the home.

A good investor client will hire you to market the home for him when it's been renovated, and if he expects a discount in your listing fee, that's reasonable. I consider myself part of the team - if I can help make money for the investor by reducing my fee, he can afford to buy more properties and is more likely to be loyal to me.

Some investors are a little more trouble. They are...indecisive. They know the house is a good deal, but they just aren't ready to make an offer. However, they don't want you telling your other investor clients about it just yet. They make ridiculous offers with 90-day closings and three-week inspection periods. They freely admit to being bottom-feeders and are hoping that eventually they'll find sellers who are desperate enough to give away their homes. And, eventually, they do get their house. But not until you've wasted hours of time and gallons of gas, written dozens of unacceptable offers and generally embarrassed yourself in the real estate community (at least that's what it feels like).

If you do ever put a home under contract with an investor like this, he will probably try to sell the home himself after renovation, mainly because he spent too much money and time renovating it and can't afford to pay you. Let him do it - he will likely need to overprice the home to break even and will be difficult to work with.

Something to keep in mind if you're working with a first-time fix-n-flipper: first projects are rarely money makers for the investor and you need to tell him that. He won't believe you, but in the majority of cases, you will be the only one who walks away with a paycheck. Inexperienced renovators always underestimate the cost and time involved in the renovations and often forget to factor in the monthly cost of holding the property. They will be lucky to just break even, but hopefully they consider their first project as an educational experience (see, it's not only real estate agents who have these).

FINDING GOOD PROJECTS FOR YOUR AMATEUR INVESTORS

Homes advertised as "fix-up's" are generally too awful for the average amateur investor. If you suspect your investor is more of a "paint and carpet" kind of guy, here are six smart ways to find him good projects.

1. **Grandma's House**
   "Original-owner" homes are some of the best projects. They are usually well maintained, but they just don't appeal to the Pottery Barn crowd. With relatively minor upgrades (exposing hardwood floors, using trendy paint colors, etc.) these homes can be quickly flipped for a tidy profit.

2. **"Sleepers"**
   If a home is in an excellent location, but hasn't sold in a reasonable amount of time, look for the reason. Perhaps there is a problem with the home that the market perceives as insurmountable. Examples might be awkward floor plans, strong smoke smells, lack of a second bathroom or

an antiquated heating system. The home is probably not being marketed to investors, and the retail buyers who are looking at it aren't responding emotionally to the home, or are overwhelmed by the "insurmountable challenge."

3. **Market Timing**

Many, if not all, markets have a "selling season". It might be a four-to-six-month period during the year when most of the annual market appreciation takes place. In Denver, we have what I call Spring Fever. Sometime between January and March, buyers come out of hiding and listings start to sell quickly. During this Spring Fever, prices appreciate and by June, there is a noticeable increase in the average sales price of homes. For example, if you have a neighborhood that hasn't quite "broken through" the $300,000 barrier, by the end of the rush, there will be several sales in the low three hundreds.

The rush slows down on the Fourth of July and the market is somewhat dead until Thanksgiving. The tail end of this slow period is a great time to buy a home to renovate. Sellers are nervous (thus motivated) and the market just feels lousy. Your investor can work on his project during the first few months of the rush and be ready for market at the height of the selling season.

4. **Sellers Buying New Construction**

In an appreciating market, one creative way to obtain good properties is to find homeowners who are purchasing a new construction home, but have a home to sell. Your investor can offer to buy the seller's current home at a reasonable discount, and allow the homeowner to continue living in the house until she is ready to move into the new home. By the time your investor takes possession of the property, it should have appreciated nicely.

5. **Poor Renovations**

Sometimes your amateur investor can take advantage of another amateur investor's mistakes. Perhaps the home was renovated poorly - and it shows. Or perhaps the investor selected drab colors and finishes and the home simply doesn't evoke any emotion. Maybe there was one problem the investor decided not to address and should have. The seller may not have enough room to negotiate much, but every once in a while you'll find one who is desperate to unload.

6. **Newer Construction**

Many homes built within the last 15 years are showing signs of wear. Most already feel dated (think about oak cabinets from the early 90's), but they're still good, solid homes. You won't be worrying about sewer lines or ancient furnaces and shouldn't have to do a major overhaul on the home's floor plan to bring it up to today's standards. Most investors are not competing against you yet (they're hot after the charming older homes), and none of these homes have been updated. So, if you can get a good price on a ten-year-old home, perhaps talk your investor into renting it for a few more years (assuming an appreciating market), then go in and cherry it out. Add the granite counters (if that's still vogue), Ralph Lauren paint, get rid of the brass light fixtures and hardware, add six-panel wood doors. Make it a Pottery Barn home that young, hip buyers will fall in love with.

Just make darn sure that your finished price will be within the neighborhood's value, or just slightly above. In a tract home subdivision, it's nearly impossible to get an appraiser to appraise a home higher than the recent highest sale, regardless of the improvements your client has made. In other words, if the market value of similar homes without updating is $235,000, don't try to sell your client's home for $270,000 and expect it to appraise.

Many amateur investors get excited about foreclosures and HUD homes. I chose not to involve myself in the foreclosure or HUD market, but you should at least take a class so you can decide for yourself. If your A+ investor client wants to do foreclosures or HUDs, at least you will be able to speak intelligently to him and hopefully get the listing when he sells. Of course, if you want to create a niche for yourself, foreclosures and HUDs are a great place to start.

BAD PROJECTS FOR INVESTORS

Some new investors get so excited about the prospect of fixing & flipping that they get impatient waiting for the right project. They'll want to jump on any fix-up project that comes along, whether or not it's a good project for them. As a new agent working with an investor, you might be impatient as well - after all, you're working your backside off for this guy, showing him properties, writing low offers and doing market research, and you'd really like to see a paycheck somewhere on the horizon. (Admittedly, this is not a soulful attitude, but we're talking reality here; at some point, you'd sure like get paid.) So, you might be tempted to support his bad decision, just to get him off your docket.

However, realize that, soul-satisfaction aside, you'll probably have to sell the renovated home your investor buys and if it's a dog, it's going to be a frustrating for both of you. Your investor will never remember that he was the one who got impatient and jumped on this crummy property; no, he'll blame you, especially as his project languishes on the market and the mortgage payments start eating away at his profit.

Here are some poor prospects for your investor:

1. **A "Fatally Flawed" Location**

    Don't ever let your investor take a chance on location. If the home has a locational "fatal flaw," such as close proximity to a noisy highway or train tracks, or is on the same block as an apartment building, low-income housing or an auto-repair shop, don't let him buy it. This is not to say that he shouldn't buy in a "marginal" neighborhood - as long as he doesn't over-improve the home, there are always buyers for renovated homes, in all price ranges, and not every investor can afford the "best" neighborhoods. But no matter how nicely your investor remodels the home, he can never overcome a location objection. It's just not worth the risk for either of you.

2. **A "Fatally Flawed" Floor Plan or Yard**

    Other than location, there are other fatal flaws that make a home a poor investment. A home with an awkward floor plan (if your investor can't or won't fix it) will still be awkward and difficult to sell no matter how nicely it is renovated. For example, a one bedroom or otherwise un-family-friendly home is always a tough sell. (Never advise an investor to eliminate bedrooms in the interest of creating larger rooms unless there are plenty of bedrooms to spare!) A home with an obvious addition (or two or three) is risky, as is a home that feels choppy or maze-like.

3. **Structural Damage**

Unless your investor is willing to professionally address and correct structural issues in a home, stay clear. And by "address and correct," I don't mean "paint over." Sloping floors, crooked doorways or cracking plaster will cause buyers to go screaming for the door. Even in a 150-year old Victorian, buyers will not usually overlook a structural problem. Even if they do, their buyer agent (or their parents!) will talk them out of purchasing your investor's property. However, if your investor is willing to repair structural concerns, this can be a great niche for him, as most investors are not.

4. **The Lovely Aroma of Cat Urine**

Cat-lovers, cover your eyes. The smell of cat urine is very difficult to remove, especially in older homes with cellars or crawl-spaces. Unless your investor has experience removing cat smell and is certain he can remove it, you should advise against purchasing a home with any odor of cat. If he cannot remove the smell, the home will be tough to sell. Many people are allergic to cats, so besides the offensive odor, they will be concerned about the previous feline residents giving them the sniffles on a daily basis.

5. **A "Unique" Home**

In central Denver, for example, urban buyers love their Bungalows, Tudors and Victorians. They are suspicious of other styles, such as Art Deco, Contemporary or Southwest. You can argue all day about the architectural appeal of one style over another, but it won't change what the market wants. Most retail buyers are looking for something predictable; something that makes "sense" to them. Investors should stick to what they know will sell; not what they personally prefer.

6. **A Dark Home**

The vast majority of home buyers want a light, bright and cheerful home. If a home is dark because it does not allow much natural light, it's a risk, even if it feels "dramatic" or "cozy." Of course, if your investor can fix the lighting issue (e.g., adding skylights or removing awnings) this might be a terrific "sleeper" investment project for him.

7. **A Too-Small Kitchen**

An otherwise fabulous home with a too-small kitchen will never sell. Unless your investor can expand the kitchen without sacrificing the utility of the surrounding rooms, don't assume the market will overlook this flaw. It won't.

THE BENEFITS OF WORKING WITH INVESTORS

Working with investors is a fantastic learning experience. Here's what you'll get:

1. **Practice honing your pricing skills**

An investor needs to know what the market value for his renovated home will be. You may need to do multiple CMA's for him on short notice, which will sharpen your skills significantly. Do the best you can to give him an accurate range. If you haven't yet seen the quality of your investor's work, be conservative. He may tell you that he's a perfectionist, but until you know for sure, don't assume that he is.

2. **Practice writing and presenting lowball offers**

Investors want a deal and that's okay. They're not looking for their dream home; they're looking for a profit. The less they pay for the house, the more profit. Duh. Try to get them to honor the seller's needs wherever they can to get the best price. Sometimes it's embarrassing to present a low offer to the seller's agent, but you'll get used to it, especially if you work with a lot of investors.

3. **Intense familiarity with neighborhoods**

Most serious investors focus on specific neighborhoods or property types, so you will find yourself becoming the local expert in their preferred neighborhoods. Not only are you on a constant lookout for under-priced homes in these neighborhoods, you are also always looking at the sold data to help them determine whether or not a project is viable.

4. **Construction knowledge**

When your investor speaks, listen. Encourage him to tell you his plans, his concerns, his considerations. When he is evaluating a home as a potential investment property, he'll give you a great education on home construction and profitable renovation.

5. **Find properties for yourself**

There's no law that says you have to turn over great investment properties you find to your investor. If, during the course of searching for properties for him, you find something you want - go for it! Just don't put yourself in the position of bidding against him.

One negative aspect of focusing heavily on investor business is that you lose out on the *fun* of real estate. Investors don't get tears in their eyes when they close on their first home. They don't worry about offending the seller. They don't refer you to all their friends because they aren't emotional about you and if you're doing a good job, they don't want to share you. When the real estate boom in Denver subsided and the investors faded away, I started working with retail buyers again. And utterly enjoyed it. To this day, I don't actively prospect investor clients; when I run into a great deal, I just buy it myself.

Working with the Out-of-Town Buyer

Out-of-town buyers are great. Sometimes. They can also be a big headache. If they're for real (a big *if*), and in town to buy a house this weekend, you will sell them a house this weekend, if you're prepared.

Before we delve into the ins and outs of the Out-of-Town Buyer, please re-read the section in Chapter Two about my trip to Florida (Under *Learn Your Market*).

Next, go to your computer and do this little exercise:

Put yourself in the buyer's shoes. Imagine that you are contemplating a move to, let's say, Kansas City or Tallahassee (pick one you have no knowledge of). You want a nice four-bedroom home with three baths and a large yard. You'd like to be close to a golf course and spend no more than $250,000.

Do a preliminary online search for homes in your target area. You can use www.Realtor.com, or just search for "Kansas City/Tallahassee Real Estate" and find a good search engine. Enter your parameters (bedrooms = at least 4, bathrooms = at least 3, etc.).

What did you find? Are you confused? Probably. If you don't know anything about a city, it's nearly impossible to sort through listings on your own. You need help.

So, as a retail buyer, what would you do next? I'd probably go back to my "Kansas City (or Tallahassee) Real Estate" search and find a few agents who look good to me (for whatever reason). I'd send e-mails to four or five of them, asking if they'd be interested in helping me out with my relocation. Of my four or five inquiries, I'd expect responses back from two.

What sort of questions would you have for the agent(s)?

> "Are you interested in working with me?"
> "Here are my parameters, what do you recommend?"
> "What areas offer good appreciation potential? Why?"
> "Can you recommend a few good lenders?"
> "In my price range, can I live near a golf course?"
> "Will you send me some listings?"

How would you select the agent to honor with your business? You would probably pick the agent who was the most responsive, the most knowledgeable and the most excited about your relocation. Agree? If so, realize that this is how your out-of-town prospects are going to evaluate you...your responsiveness, your market knowledge and your enthusiasm.

That little exercise was a reality check. Never forget how vulnerable and dependent on you out-of-town buyers are. They need you to be opinionated. They need you to be knowledgeable. They need you to be responsive before, during and after their trip. They will be high maintenance—before, during and after their visit.

Types of Out-of-Town Buyers

You will work with many types of out-of-town buyers during your career. All deserve your respect and attention, but it will serve you well to discern which ones are "For Real" and which ones will probably "poof" on you. The best type of out-of-town buyer is, of course, the buyer who is definitely moving to your town in the near future. Let's call him the Type One Buyer. He should be a top priority for you. The second type (Type Two) is the Rent-for-Now "Buyer", who is definitely moving, but plans to rent for a while. If you manage rentals as well as home sales, this type may also be a top priority. If you don't manage rental properties, I'd probably call her a medium priority. The Lookie-Loo (Type Three) is thinking about moving to your town, but is considering other locations as well. If she has definite plans to visit your town, she is also a medium priority. Last, we have the Investor (Type Four) who has heard about your booming real estate market and wants a piece of it. This type is a tough call. As a new agent, you should probably work with Type Fours, for the experience if nothing else.

We'll discuss each type fully.

Type One - The Sure Thing

They have a job, they've sold their current home, they need to buy a house. Preferably from you. You must be prepared for these buyers! They're not messing around and they don't want to waste their time. Once they're in town, you won't have time to do much market research or previewing. Clear your calendar the week/weekend of their visit. Get help if you need it. Preview, preview, preview, preview. Preview everything that might interest them. Take good notes. Get a list from them of homes they've seen online that interest them. Preview those too.

Show only the best properties, but show as many as you can. These buyers need to look at houses until they drop. Ten to fifteen homes in one day, if they're up for it. If at all possible, schedule your first trip in the afternoon so that your day is by necessity abbreviated. This way, you can get a feel for how quickly they go through a home, which will help you plan your full day tomorrow. On the other hand, if they have a young child in tow, ask them how much time to allot.

Don't plan to show too many homes in one neighborhood. If they don't like the neighborhood, they won't want to see any more inventory there. During the process, they will (hopefully) zero in on a few choice areas and you can plan your next day accordingly.

It's not uncommon for relocating buyers to completely revise their search criteria in the middle of their visit, so stay flexible. I once had out-of-town buyers who switched gears from Charming Old Denver to Suburban Tract Home Hell four times during their six-day visit. That was their right, but it was tough on me. Tract Home Hell is not my forte and I had a terrible time getting around without the chance to preview. However, they knew that I was an urban specialist, and luckily I had proven myself competent and confident in the urban neighborhoods before we headed off to foreign lands together.

Brush up on your Fair Housing speech for when they ask you about the safety, desirability or investment potential of a neighborhood. Because they will. Be as helpful as you can without risking your license. Be prepared with website addresses for local crime statistics and public school demographics since these are sensitive topics, and can get you in trouble.

If they are planning to buy a house on this visit, have your lender on alert. The buyers will likely have lots of financing questions as they start to narrow down their list to two or three homes. When they find the home they want to buy, they will want all kinds of market data from you to help them determine their offer price. Yes, your opinion will be welcomed, but you will need to be able to back it up with solid data. Regardless of the great rapport you've built with these buyers, they are still suspicious of you. They don't know the market at all and don't want to make a mistake.

They may very well want to make a lowball offer. Out-of-town buyers almost always do. If you strongly disagree due to the current state of the market in your area, express your opinion, calmly, professionally, and then shut up. If they insist, cheerfully write it up. Remember, they need to buy a house this weekend more than you need to sell a house this weekend, but if you get into an argument with them over offer price, they may abandon you and call up one of the other agents they spoke with before choosing you.

Put yourself in their shoes. They're nervous. They don't want to make a mistake. If their offer is countered or rejected, they may be willing to pay full price, but they need to feel they gave it their best shot first. With your 100% support, they can more easily make the right decision for themselves.

If you successfully put a home under contract for these buyers, you can proceed as normal toward the closing. Well, sort of. The buyers may not be in town for the inspection or even the closing. You'll need to do a lot of hand-holding, especially during the inspection period. You'll likely need to help them gather estimates for repairs, even meet contractors at the home.

Do a good job for these buyers and you'll be rewarded with many referrals. Think about it - what's the first question they'll be asked at their new job? "How did the move go?" If you were great, you'll get some good press.

Type Two - The "Rent-for-Now" Buyer

Again, if you work in property management as well as real estate sales, go headlong after this buyer/renter. If not, it still won't hurt you to spend some time with him. If he's owned a home before, he may reconsider his decision to rent once he sees the rental inventory. In any case, he won't want to rent forever and may be ready to buy within six months.

His first priority when he visits your town will be to secure housing, so let him explore his rental options. Be cheerfully available to him to answer his questions about what he's seeing. If he seems interested and "for real," offer to take him on a little tour of neighborhoods you think he'd consider buying in. Show him some homes if he asks. Your goal is to build rapport and get your business card in his hand so he'll call you in six months. Get his new address, put him in your SOI database and schedule some follow-up calls.

Type Three - The Lookie-Loo Buyer

Frankly, this buyer is probably a time-waster. But in your first year - you know by now how I feel about wasting time. It won't kill you to spend some time with her. Build an e-mail rapport with her, be cheerfully responsive to her dozens of questions about your city. If she actually makes a trip to your town, you'll need to spend a lot of time with her, just as you would with the Type One buyers. Don't make a half-assed effort with her - if she falls in love with a home you show her, she just might escalate her plans and move next month. I've seen it happen! If she's definitely not in a position to move for several months or more, spend a day with her and play it by ear after that.

But stay in touch - she's probably an online shopper and will likely talk to other agents during her information-gathering period. Don't bother her with a buyer agency agreement or anything like that; just strive to be her best resource for information.

Type Four - The Investor

This buyer is a high-maintenance, high-risk prospect. However, if he pans out, he could be a gold mine.

Imagine yourself as this buyer. You hear a rumor that a certain area is experiencing double-digit appreciation. You have some money to invest and would like to buy some real estate in a growing market. You get all revved up one morning and start e-mailing brokers in your new favorite city.

You tell them that you're an investor and are interested in purchasing a home or two in their city. For investment. No, you've never been there, but you've heard it's appreciating rapidly. You'd like the agent to send you some listings of under-market properties for your review. If you like the look of the homes, you'll come visit - sometime.

Most experienced agents would ignore you - I probably would. A hot market is no secret - plenty of local investors (including real estate agents) are watching the market closely for "under-market properties". Great deals are not sitting around on the MLS waiting for an out-of-town investor to review at his leisure.

That said, I recently was contacted by an out-of-town investor looking to purchase several condominiums in a particular complex. Because he already knew exactly what he wanted, it was pretty easy. I previewed all the available units, took digital photos of every single room in every single condo and e-mailed them to him with my comments. He selected three to make offers on, we got two and he closed without ever seeing the properties personally. As an introverted real estate agent, this was a perfect setup for me! No driving-the-buyer-all-over-town small talk required!

Whether or not to work with an out-of-town investor is a judgment call on your part. If it's a learning experience, it's not a waste of time, but working with an unmotivated, out-of-town investor comes pretty close, regardless of how much you learn. If the investor has no idea what he wants, no familiarity with your city and no firm plans to visit, I'd probably let him go. (Actually, I'd probably refer him to someone hungrier than I am.) If your market is truly hot, you'll easily find plenty of local investors to go after.

On the other hand, if the out-of-town investor is familiar with your city, has some local connections (friends, family) and is planning to visit next month, go ahead and play along for a while. Some of my best clients and sources of referrals have started out just this way.

4

The Proper Care & Feeding of Sellers
Part I ~ Before You Go to Market...

Creating a Listing Presentation, Pricing Homes
to Sell and Negotiating Your Commission

Your First Listing Presentation

Yahoo! You have your first listing appointment. Yikes! You have your first listing appointment!

Thinking back, I recall that I was a little embarrassed by the boilerplate material that my Big Name company provided me to use on listings. I thought it was patronizing to the client and didn't reflect who I really was. I don't think I ever used it, even on my very first listing appointment. If the listing proposal material that is provided by your company resonates with you, by all means use it.

Instead, I created my own written listing proposal. It says what I want it to say, how I want to say it, and I feel that it assumes a level of intelligence on the part of my seller prospect. Home sellers may sit through three or more listing proposals before they hire an agent, so I feel it is my duty to cut out the fluff and propaganda, and get directly to the point - that is, what I think the house is worth, what I'm going to do to sell it and how much I'm going to charge.

Some agents take the reduction of fluff and propaganda to the extreme. I've seen more than one Top Dog agent race out the door, late for a listing appointment, a pile of MLS printouts in hand. This is their listing proposal. Clearly it works for them and they must have the confidence and charisma to pull it off, although I think it's disrespectful to the client.

Not being particularly charismatic, I need the crutch and support of a well-prepared listing proposal. My prospects are always impressed with how professional and thorough my presentations are and I know they appreciate the time I take putting them together.

My written listing proposal consists of two major sections. The first (the marketing proposal) is an introduction to me, my services and my fees. The second is the market analysis or CMA.

SECTION ONE (THE MARKETING PROPOSAL)

Marketing Services:	A summary of the services I provide my selling clients. Includes both pre-contract (marketing) and post-contract (closing) services.
My Fee:	A one page description of my listing fee.
Samples of Marketing:	Internet pages, color brochures, newspaper ads, etc.
My Bragging Rights:	A list of homes sold, awards, newspaper clippings.

SECTION TWO (THE CMA)

Your Property:	A printout of the county assessor page for their home. I also include the prior MLS listing of the home if it has been listed in the last three years.
Current Competition:	*Comparable Listings* - similar homes for sale in the immediate neighborhood.

Other Competition - similar homes for sale outside of the immediate neighborhood, but comparable in appeal.

Recent Sales:

All Recent Neighborhood Sales (not just the comparable homes).
Recent Comparable Sales - the ten or so homes that have recently sold in the same general price range as the prospect.
Most Comparable Sales - the three or so homes that you will be using to price this home.

Pending Sales:

A simple list of the homes showing as "under contract."

Expired Listings:

The comparable homes that did not sell.

Estimate of Market Value - Check with your broker for the various CMA programs that are available in your market. You will want to provide a pricing recommendation backed up by solid data, in an easy-to-understand format.*

Estimated Cost of Sale - Otherwise known as a "net sheet." To calculate the estimated cost of sale, you take the projected sales price less the commission and any other fees the seller pays such as a title policy, recording fees, closing fees or HOA transfer fees. Your broker can help you with the particulars in your market. (If you have not yet determined a market value for the home, you can still do a net sheet. Just use a nice round number and make sure your prospect knows it's for "illustrative purposes" only.)

You may choose not to include this in your initial listing proposal because you can't really accurately price a home until you've seen the interior. If you are making your presentation to the seller at the same time you are seeing the home for the first time, just tell the seller you will get back to him right away with your pricing recommendation.

A sample listing presentation template in its entirety is available on my website, www.sellwithsoul.com.

You do not have to review all this data line by line with the seller. You just want to show the seller you have done your homework, and that you are a professional. He can review it at his leisure. Even if he really doesn't care about all the market data, he will appreciate the effort you took preparing it for him.

Once you get the hang of it, you'll be able to put most of the presentation together in your sleep. The trick is knowing your software well enough to trust the data it gives you. Nothing is worse than driving to your prospect's home for the listing interview and seeing For Sale signs in front of comparable homes that didn't make your list. Bad, very bad for your confidence.

PRICING THE HOME

One of the most important duties of your job is to properly price your listings for market. Getting listings is one thing, selling them is another. Sure, it's fun to see your name on a sign in a yard, but yard signs don't pay the bills. There is a right way to price a home, which involves a thorough review of the market - the active competition, the recent sales and the expired listings. The wrong way is to allow your seller to dictate the price. Not that you don't want her input, but you need to know in your heart what the right price range is and be able to defend it.

You know how they say that you learn the most from the challenges in your life? The good stuff rarely teaches you anything and the most valuable lessons come from your mistakes and mis-steps. I could take up the rest of this book telling you why and how not to take overpriced listings, but you will do it anyway. We all do. I have three overpriced listings on my books now. However, as you mature in your real estate career, you will learn how to say no - to either turn down a listing or tactfully convince your seller to see things your way.

Believe it or not, there are lots of Old School agents out there who don't particularly care if their listings sell or not. They just want to blanket the town with their signs and will do whatever it takes to procure yet another listing, which often includes overpricing their listings to "win" the seller's business. However, what they forget is that, as licensed professional real estate agents, it is their duty to be honest and straightforward with their sellers about market value. Our job as real estate agents is not to make friends because we are the highest bidder. Sellers are depending on us and our recommendations in order to make important decisions.

It's easy to forget this. To forget that we are hired by sellers to do a job, part of which might include telling them something they don't want to hear. In my opinion (and the opinion of your real estate commission), misleading a seller with respect to the marketability of her home is unethical. Ignorance of the market is no excuse. If you don't know (and are not willing to learn) the nuances of a particular market, you have no business going on that listing appointment. Real estate is not about you and your needs! Don't forget this!

The "Art" of Pricing Homes

Between you and me, pricing a home is an art, not a science. While there certainly are objective parameters to help you price a home (square footage, bedrooms, baths, lot size, etc.), the final buying decision is almost always based on emotion. If there are two identical homes on the same block for sale and one smells good, looks good and feels good, and the other is smoky, poorly furnished and hard to show, there *is* a difference in market value, which may be hard to objectively demonstrate.

However, your clients and prospects look at you as the expert. In reality, there is no way to accurately and scientifically place a value on a home; a lot depends on market conditions (that week!), luck, and even the weather. But sellers understandably want you (the expert) to tell them exactly

JENNIFER'S $0.02...

I firmly believe that if you don't work with buyers on a regular basis, you don't have the expertise to accurately price homes for market. Many experienced agents snottily declare that they Don't Work With Buyers - they only handle listings and hire buyer agents to show homes. I know a few agents in my area who are huge listers and have never shown or previewed one of my listings. I don't understand how they can claim to be the neighborhood experts when they don't know the competition and don't have an understanding of how buyers think.

what their home is worth. So, I do my best to give them as much hard data as I can to justify my pricing recommendation.

WHAT IF YOU UNDERPRICE A HOME?

Every once in a while a seller will convince me to "try" a higher listing price than I recommend. When I do, I always regret it. That's 100% of the time. So why do I do it? Because I'm afraid of *underpricing* the home. Believe me, there's nothing fun about receiving multiple offers on a brand new listing (unless that's normal for your market). Your seller is initially excited, but soon enough he'll be looking askance at you with the unspoken (if you're lucky) accusation that you underpriced his home. Never mind that he probably got a higher sales price than he expected, never mind that his worries about languishing on the market were unfounded - you cost him money.

This has happened to me twice. Both times, I was confident that my pricing recommendation was accurate, but for whatever reason, the market responded to the listing more positively than I expected. Fortunately, both times, the homes sold in bidding wars for much higher than the listed price. However, it was uncomfortable enough for me to still question myself every time I price a home. In fact, I often breathe a sigh of relief 48 hours after putting a home on the market that it didn't sell in a bidding war.

I'll never forget the scolding I received the last time I underpriced a home. My market analysis showed a value of $408,000 to $419,000, but the house showed so well, I agreed to try $425,000. The first day on the market, we had eight showings and four offers. Ouch.

We put the home under contract at $441,000. My sellers got everything they wanted, including a rent-back agreement that heavily favored the sellers. I figured they would be happy. I should have known better.

A few days later, I had to apologize to my seller for some miscommunication with my showing service and during my apology phone call, my seller said, "And Jennifer, we've never discussed how you grossly underpriced our home. Obviously you didn't do your homework and I'm disappointed in you. Just so you know, we don't intend to fix anything at the inspection or be flexible in any way with these buyers." Talk about a buzz-kill.

At the risk of sounding like sour grapes, it's impossible to explain to sellers that, had they priced the home higher, they would probably have ended up at the same sales price, only after a longer marketing period and more disruption in their lives. They don't understand how painful it is to fall into the death spiral where you can't reduce the price fast enough as the listing gets stale.

My recommendation? You're better off taking the chance of underpricing a home than overpricing it. Keep in mind that in ten years, I only underpriced two homes. But I overpriced plenty and everyone suffered. No one wins when a home is overpriced. Especially not the seller.

Real estate is not always fun. But most of the time it is.

Five Steps to the Right Price

If you are a new agent, be prepared to spend several hours on your first listing presentations. As you gain expertise, you should be able to put together a market analysis in an hour or two. But in the beginning, the more time you spend in preparation, the more confident you will be going to your appointment. Here are the steps to follow each and every time you price a home for market.

1. Drive by the Home

It doesn't matter how well you know the subject property's neighborhood, you must not skip this step. More often than not you will be surprised by what you see. A gas station across the alley, an overbuilt home next door blocking the light, a hideous enclosed sun porch...or perhaps the home suffers from excessive highway noise. *Drive around the block to identify the other homes for sale in the immediate area. You must know the price and status of these homes before you step foot into your listing prospect's home.*

One evening I had a listing appointment for a home outside of my comfort zone. I had never been anywhere near the neighborhood, but I was an "experienced" agent at this point and figured I could wing it. I prepared my market analysis without driving by the home and was fairly confident as I drove to my appointment. My confidence started to fade as I saw lots of For Sale signs within a few blocks of my prospect. None of these properties were shown on my market analysis and I had no idea how they were priced. I was a little bit early, so I frantically started calling the listing offices of these homes, trying to get as much information as I could so I wouldn't look like a complete idiot with my prospect. As you can imagine, all I managed to accomplish was to increase my anxiety to the point I considered canceling the appointment all together.

What I did instead was take out the market analysis section of my listing presentation with the promise to return the next day with the information "now that I'd seen their home." I didn't get the listing, and I suspect it was due partly to my lack of confidence upon meeting the seller. Moral of the story - you must be confident in the quality and thoroughness of your market data.

2. Find Your Market Data

This might be harder than you think. In many MLS systems, it can be difficult to isolate the homes in a given area that you need to use as comparable properties. Depending on your city, you can use North/South - East/West boundaries, neighborhood names, school district or zip codes. However, many times these pieces of information are subject to mistakes or omissions in input by the listing agent or the office staff. Your goal is to produce a comprehensive list of every single home that is available or has recently sold within the area of the subject property. It is embarrassing and deflating when your prospect asks you about a recent sale down the street that you don't know anything about. Your credibility and confidence take an unneeded hit.

In the Denver market, for example, the best way I have found to search for comparable properties is to search by street name and address number. In my MLS search, I input the street names of the ten streets to the east and west of my subject property, along with address numbers ten blocks north and south (that's the way the Denver grid is laid

> **CAUTION!**
> *You need to realize that the MLS is loaded with mistakes and erroneous information. Either the information is entered by the listing agents themselves (who by nature aren't usually detail fanatics) or by the office manager, who hasn't seen the home.*

out). I get all the homes in the immediate area and am not dependent on the listing agent's accurate data input. Errors abound in MLS listings, but you can usually count on the property street name and address number being correct.

If your MLS or your subject area's layout makes this search strategy imprac
try to find a search parameter that is not dependent upon the listing age.
discretion. Never use the neighborhood name if the listing agent has any
control over that field. Given the opportunity, agents will always try to
"upgrade" the location of their listings to a swankier neighborhood.

3. Preview All Active Listings Competing with the Subject Property

Don't miss any homes in the immediate area...and fan out as time permits.
Take notes on the listing printout. If you have already seen the interior of
the subject home, rate the properties against it–(e.g., "Nicer than," "Better
location than," etc.). Your seller prospect may have already seen these homes
too, either at open houses or neighborhood events, so you need to be familiar
with the interiors of as many nearby listings as you can.

4. Print Out and Drive by the Solds in the Immediate Area

Since these homes have already sold, obviously you can't preview them.
Do the best you can with the exterior appearance and the MLS comments.
Note which homes are most similar in appeal and location.

5. Review Your Data and Determine the Market Value Range

The results of your research will be entered into the Market Analysis
section of your listing presentation. As you are preparing the analysis, you will
start to narrow in on a price range for the property. It just happens naturally.
This is why I can't imagine having anyone else prepare my market analyses. It
is your job as the real estate broker to know the market and to be comfortable
educating your seller on current market values. The process of preparing a
market analysis is as much for you as for the client.

Put it all together and Voilá! You have completed your first CMA!

THE TWO MOST INTIMIDATING CONVERSATIONS IN REAL ESTATE

There are two sensitive topics to be discussed in a listing presentation.
One is your commission. I'll cover that topic fully a little later. The other is
your pricing recommendation for the home.

Discussing Price with Your Seller Prospect

Most of the time, your seller prospect thinks his home is worth more than you do. Or, even if he agrees with you (in theory) he still wants to test the market, just in case you're both wrong. Popular seller arguments are:

"I don't want to leave money on the table."

"I'm not in a hurry."

"But I need $xx,xxx to make it worth selling."

"Buyers can always make an offer."

You will hear these statements over and over. In fact, when you sell your own home, you'll laugh at yourself when you hear your very own voice making the same arguments.

Let's counter each objection individually.

"I don't want to leave money on the table"
My Response:
I understand and I don't want to give away your money. However, the risk of leaving money on the table is slim, almost non-existent. If we accidentally or even intentionally underprice your home, the market will recognize it as a bargain and your home will sell at market value, even if that market value is higher than our asking price. In my ten years of selling real estate, I have only underpriced two homes and both times the home sold above the asking price with multiple offers.

"But I'm not in a hurry!"
My Response:
Our goal needs to be a 30-day sale - that's what we're shooting for. The quicker your home sells, the higher your sales price will be. After 30 days on the market, listings become stale and are considered fair game for low-ball offers by buyers. There is an energy in a new listing that quickly fades after a month. Would you be willing to pay full price for a home that has been on the market for 63 days? For 122 days?

"I need $xxx,xxx to make it worth selling" or "I won't sell if I can't walk away with $xx,xxx in my pocket."

My Response:

I understand. So here's an idea. Why don't we hold off on listing the home right now and, when the market improves, we'll list it then? I'd be happy to stay in touch with you in the meantime and when I see enough appreciation in the market I'll let you know right away.

(This is a brilliant strategy. It subtly tells the seller that you are willing to walk away from his listing without coming right out and saying so. You aren't beating up the seller by telling him (again) that his price is too high, just that the timing might not be quite right. Somehow this strategy elevates you to a consultant status rather than a desperate salesperson. Don't worry, he won't want to wait to sell his home unless he truly isn't motivated - in which case, you probably don't even want the listing.)

"Buyers can always make an offer."

My Response:

That's true. But here's the problem with that strategy. Buyer agents try to show homes to their buyers that fit their needs for features and price. If we are overpriced compared to the other homes the buyers are looking at, then the buyers who see your home won't buy it even at a lower price. For example, if a buyer's requirements are four bedrooms and a two-car garage and your house is three bedrooms with no garage, and in his price range there are plenty of four bedroom homes, he won't want your house regardless of price. He can afford the house that suits him and he won't make an offer on yours. Conversely, the buyer who would be satisfied with your three-bedroom, garage-less home won't ever see it because it's priced out of the price range he gave his buyer agent. Buyer agents don't like to waste their time showing homes that their buyer can't afford. So, it's unlikely that the Perfect Buyer for your home would ever even see it, much less make an offer on it.

In this market, there are more buyers than sellers. Your listing needs to stand out from the crowd in order to sell, that is, it needs to be better than the competition to motivate a buyer to make a (good) offer. This means that your home needs to show better and/or be priced a little lower than other comparable homes. It needs to excite the market, not just be "fairly priced."

93

Your responses are best delivered with the attitude that the question/objection is an excellent one, one that you've never heard before. Respond thoughtfully and respectfully. Bringing your seller around to your point of view without his realizing that you led him there is truly in his best interest. Try to put yourself in a seller's shoes. He wants the highest price for his home, of course, who wouldn't? But he

CAUTION!
Use the above responses judiciously. You don't want to antagonize your seller by appearing argumentative or implying that he's an idiot. If you get all four objections in one conversation, perhaps just address one or two in detail and simply smile sympathetically as if to say, "I know, I know, what can we do?" at the others.

may not understand that the best way to get the highest price is to price the home fairly at the very beginning. It's up to you to make him see this without alienating him.

If you are a born salesperson, this may come naturally to you. Good for you. If you're like the rest of us, it will take practice and a confidence in your market knowledge. As a new or newer agent, you probably don't have that yet. It will come and is something to look forward to.

What *will* help you tremendously is to truly feel in your heart that you don't need this listing. That the seller is not doing you a favor by hiring you - you are bringing your expertise to the table and if the seller does not agree with your professional analysis of the situation, that's fine with you! When a seller sees that you're willing to stick to your guns and cheerfully walk away from his business, his attitude toward you shifts - you'll find that he begins to see you as the expert - it's a beautiful thing. And if he doesn't, it's a listing you probably don't want, no matter how desperate for business you think you are.

Negotiating Your Commission

Fourteen months into my career, I listed a home (the seller picked the price and the 4% commission) and I marketed it hard (it was my second or third listing ever). It was an adorable home on a great lot and it sold quickly at full price. We got through the inspection with no problems. Then, on the day before I was leaving town for my honeymoon - the house didn't appraise. The appraiser's value was about $8,000 lower than the sales price and, on paper, he was right. "Adorable," as you may know, doesn't impress an appraiser.

I didn't know what to do. I really didn't. I argued, I begged, I tried to charm the appraiser, and he was sympathetic, but I didn't give him anything to work with. It appeared that my seller was going to have to reduce her sales price by $8,000 to get the house to closing. She was not amused. At that point, she made the comment, "Well, I guess I got what I paid for," referring to me and my low commission. And you know what? She was right. I didn't have the experience to solve the problem.

But a more experienced agent did. The appraiser (God bless him) took pity on me (after all I was getting married in a few days) and called another agent he knew who did a lot of business in the neighborhood. The other agent was familiar with my listing (I'm sure he interviewed for it) and was able to give the appraiser information about the sold comparables that enabled him to raise his appraised value to the sales price. Whew! Right?

Yes, I dodged a bullet. The home closed and we all moved on. An interesting epilogue to this story - the owner of the home went on to get her real estate license and is quite successful. I'm certain that when people ask her why she went into real estate, she tells them the story about her clueless real estate agent (me) and how she knew she could do better.

So here's my point...

If you are a new real estate salesperson, I don't care how enthusiastic, how smart, how cute, how motivated you are, you are not as qualified to handle the marketing and sale of a home as a good, experienced real estate agent. Now, you might be more qualified than a bad experienced agent, and there are plenty of those. But, be honest, if you were going to hire someone to sell your home (or invest your money, design your logo or walk your dog), would you really prefer someone who has never done it before over an experienced professional?

Every agent goes through a rookie year. Somehow we convince people to give us the listing on their homes, and, in most cases, everything comes out okay.

At the end of the year, you can breathe a sign of relief that you'll never have to be a rookie real estate agent again.

But until then, here's what I think new agents should do. You need listings - you need the inventory to attract buyers and you need the experience. Buy them. The listings, I mean. No, I don't mean you should overprice them (although you'll do that too). Be the lowest bidder on your commission. Your broker might not agree with me, but here's why I think it's a good idea.

First, it's fair to the seller. You don't have the experience or expertise of a 5-year, 10-year or 25-year agent. Don't argue with me, you don't. If a reasonable listing fee in your area is 6%, you aren't worth that yet. Maybe you're worth 4%. Maybe you should even consider working for free for a while; after all, most professions require you to actually pay money to learn a trade, don't they? Ever heard of internships or residencies or apprenticeships? Perhaps you could charge your sellers a marketing fee of, say, $300, which will cover your advertising costs.

You could creatively market yourself as a first-year real estate agent building a business at a discounted commission. You don't have to come right out and tell sellers that you're learning the ropes at their expense, but they'll realize that, and might even cut you a little slack. After all, if they want a more experienced agent, they can pay for him.

Second, it will help you build your confidence to charge more when you feel you're worth it. I took a lot of 4% commissions my first few years because I didn't have the confidence in my knowledge or my competency to negotiate a higher fee. And I figured a little paycheck is better than no paycheck. Now I have no problem stating my fee and explaining why I am worth it, and I usually get the listing - if I want it.

So, how do you talk your broker into this strategy? Maybe this will be the first test of your sales skills—make a commitment to your broker that you'll take five listings at 4% (or even free) and then you'll be more comfortable charging a market-rate fee. It might even encourage you to get out there and get those listings over with so you can make some real money!

How to Completely Eliminate Any Fee Negotiation

Once you're past your first five listings and you're ready to charge a market-rate fee, consider incorporating this great strategy that I used in my business.

Offer your sellers a choice in fee structure, rather than one fee that they suspect is negotiable. I think sellers are just as uncomfortable discussing a brokerage fee as you are presenting it. They know they're supposed to negotiate the commission and they want to feel they got the best deal. So, you are automatically starting off the relationship with the seller as an adversary instead of a partner.

Give your clients an option. They can pay your full commission (let's say 6%), which includes all marketing, advertising and services you describe in your proposal. If you don't sell the home, you don't get paid. Alternatively, they can pay you a reduced commission (let's say 5.2%) with a non-refundable $300 marketing fee, paid at the time of listing. Their choice. Present these options to them up front, maybe before you even meet. It's Sales Tactic #131, "Give people an alternative rather than a straight yes or no proposition."

I think this way is fair to everyone. If you do the math, you'll see that the 5.2% + $300 option will save the seller money and put fewer dollars in your pocket at the end of the day. But the majority of your marketing expenses are paid up front, so if the home does not sell, you've only wasted your time, not your money. And sellers will understand that. You're sharing the risk with your sellers, thus taking a little bit less of a paycheck.

I had great feedback from my sellers on this plan. The discussion over my fee usually took place between the sellers before I even arrived for my appointment and by the time I got there, the sellers told me which plan they preferred. Done - we could move on to less adversarial topics.

When You "Double-End" a Sale...

In real estate, "double-ending" refers to selling your own listing. You "double-end the deal" by getting both sides of the commission. Yeah, it's cool. But watch out. Depending on your state law, you might be in the uncomfortable position of "representing" both parties. Parties who are natural adversaries.

Which means, by association, both parties now view you as an adversary too.

Negotiating your commission on a double-ended deal is something to discuss up front with your seller. Many savvy sellers will ask you at the time of listing if you will waive the buyer agent fee if you sell their home yourself. I always say no. They always seem surprised. Here's how I explain it to them.

"I sell real estate to earn a living. If I find a ready, willing and able buyer who is going to buy a home, I'd sure like to sell him a home and get paid for it. If I agree to reduce or waive the buyer agent commission if I bring the buyer to your home, that's a built-in incentive for me to take my buyers elsewhere. I think that's unethical. If I know that I'll make 3% for selling a buyer a house down the street, but only 1% if I sell him yours, it's going to be tempting for me to encourage him to buy the other house. And if I sell him your home, I'm doing the work of both agents, and it's only fair that I get paid for that."

I'm blunt this way; it's part of my charm. Some sellers like it, some don't. But it's my style. You will find your own. But my theory is absolutely above reproach. If you don't like my delivery, make up one that feels warm and fuzzy to you. But have an answer ready.

Now, truth be told, whenever I've double-ended a sale I have always kicked in part of my commission to make some problem go away. After all, being paid 5% or 6% on my listing is a pretty big paycheck and I'm motivated to make sure it closes.

Yet every time I've doubled-ended a sale, I've also said I'd never do it again. The money is sweet, but the sale itself is almost always ugly. Both sides are suspicious of you and your motives (perhaps with reason). Suddenly, the seller you promised your utmost loyalty to has to accept that you are assisting someone else to negotiate against him. He wonders what secrets he shared with you are now being shared with the buyer.

I double-ended my first listing. My sellers had told me early on that their bottom line was $155,000. Damned if my buyer didn't want to offer $155,000! My sellers came right out and accused me of disclosing their bottom line price to him and I can't blame them for wondering.

No matter how hard you try to be neutral, it's going to be difficult to 1) truly be neutral throughout the sale and 2) convince both parties that you are being neutral. Unless you're lucky and happen to put a cheerful seller and an easy-going buyer together, you're going to have some stressful moments.

A word of warning. If the buyer appears to be inexperienced, suspicious or otherwise difficult, I highly recommend referring him to another agent to represent him. Or, if your broker approves, bring in a more experienced agent to work with you and pay him part of the buyer agent fee. As you gain experience, double-ending listings won't be so hard, but in the beginning, it's probably a good practice to protect yourself first.

Discounting Your Commission – The "Family" Discount

Here's a shocker. Your friends and family are going to assume you will give them a discount off your "standard" commission. Here's a bigger shocker. I say, do it!

It's the way of the world and you as a real estate agent are not so darn special that you don't have to participate. When you go have drinks at the bar where your buddy is bartending, don't you figure you'll get a drink or two on the house? If your best friend sells, let's say, vinyl windows, wouldn't you assume she'd get you a "great deal"? If your sister is an accountant, would you really expect to pay her full fee to do your taxes? So why do we real estate agents get so insulted and snotty when our friends and family assume they'll get a great deal from their favorite real estate agent?

Of course, if you're developing a referral-based business, many of your customers will also be your friends and you can't cut everyone a "great deal." But don't be categorically opposed to the idea of commission discounting for special people. And making people feel special is a great way to generate good will and future referrals.

What about repeat customers and "frequent" buyers or sellers? Again, I have no problem making them feel special by reducing my fee for them. They *are* special and I can afford to cut my fee to keep them coming back.

5

The Proper Care & Feeding of Sellers
Part II ~ On The Market

Marketing, Selling and Closing Your Listings

Marketing Your Listing

So, you have the listing agreement signed! Do you know what to do next?

Assuming you work in an office (as opposed to under your own steam), your office administrator will make darn sure you have all your paperwork complete. Corporate real estate offices tend to be pretty tight on such things, so I'll bet you'll get a checklist of the required contracts and disclosures. It's likely that your listing will not see the light of the MLS until everything is reviewed and found satisfactory by the paperwork Nazi - um, sorry, the office manager. No offense to office managers, someone has to keep us in line.

Following is my checklist, complete with my commentary, of the items I have found that need to be handled during the course of the listing, outside of the typical activities regulated and monitored by your office. This list has been developed and improved over years of selling real estate and is one of the most important tools I use in my real estate practice.

CHECKLIST FOR NEW LISTINGS

(You can find the checklist without my commentary, in the Appendix or at my website www.sellwithsoul.com)

THINGS TO DO PRIOR TO MLS ENTRY

√   Get all contracts and disclosures completed and signed by seller

√   Take pictures (see below)

THINGS TO DO THE DAY OF MLS ENTRY

√   Schedule the virtual tour (see below)

√   Get the key, install the lockbox
    Make sure the key works smoothly in the lock! Don't make it hard for agents to get into the house. If your seller tells you there's a "trick" to unlocking the door, encourage the seller to have it repaired. No, insist on it.

√   Get the HOA contact information from seller
    If applicable

√   Enter your listing on to the MLS

√   Enter the listing in your contract manager program
    If you use one

√   Order "Just Listed" cards
    If your office pays for these, go ahead and order them. I do not recommend spending your own money on Just Listed/Just Sold cards, though.

√   Track the expiration date
    When a listing expires, your seller is fair game for other agents to market to. It's terribly embarrassing to hear from your seller that real estate agents are prospecting him to let him know his listing expired. Make sure you have a system to alert you a week or two ahead of time. Your office manager probably tracks this for you, but confirm.

√ Install the For Sale sign
Be sure the placement of your sign complies with any city ordinances. In Denver, it's illegal to put a sign in the "tree lawn" which is the space between the sidewalk and the street. If you do put a sign there, it will be kidnapped by the sign police and held hostage.

√ Give the seller's showing instructions to your office or showing service

√ Create and display Special Feature cards in the home
Things like "New Air Conditioner!" "Don't Miss the Walk-in Closet!" "Don't let the cats out, please!" The more Special Features you can come up with, the more your seller will love you.

√ Send a copy (e-mail or fax) of the MLS listing to seller for review

√ Call the seller when his listing is activated
This is good PR and prepares him for showings.

THINGS TO DO RIGHT AFTER MLS ENTRY

√ Deliver copies of all signed documents to your seller

√ Prepare the home brochure - send to the printer

√ Schedule the open house, put up OPEN SUNDAY rider on sign
If applicable

THINGS TO DO DURING THE FIRST WEEK OF YOUR LISTING

√ Call the HOA and complete your questionnaire
If applicable; see Chapter Eight for details on the questionnaire.

√ Pick up the home brochures, deliver to home
Don't put all the brochures in the outside box; if the lid is left open, your brochures can be ruined. Try to get your seller to help keep the box filled. If the home is vacant and you can't commit to keeping the box filled, take the brochure box down after your first batch of brochures are gone. Empty brochure boxes annoy buyers, which makes you look bad.

√ Start providing showing feedback (see below)

√ Load Internet advertising

√ E-mail web links to seller (see below)

√ Schedule Fluff & Flush visits
If the home is vacant; see below for an explanation of "Fluffing & Flushing."

√ Send first marketing package to seller (see below)

√ Call seller, "Are the showing instructions working for you?" (see below)

THINGS TO DO THROUGH-OUT THE LISTING PERIOD

√ Call to check-in every ten days

√ Fluff & flush every seven days
If the home is vacant

√ Check the status of home brochures every Thursday
You want to make sure your brochure box is full for the weekend.

√ Send market updates every three weeks

√ Prepare and schedule your six-week CMA meeting

√ Re-take your exterior photos
If the seasons have changed, update your exterior photos. If it's June, a snowy MLS photo will scream "Desperate Seller Here!" to potential buyers and agents.

* * *

Your MLS Entry

Make your MLS entries accurate, clear and appealing. You don't need to list every single feature in the written description; your goal is to inspire agents and online buyers to schedule a showing.

Compare the following two listings:

2356 King Court
> *"Stng blk; lake shops dwntwn jst min away; updts inc newr mech syst, wd flrsundr crpt, nwr fxtrs in kitch/bath, tile kitch flrs, elc blnd(?), mechs drmovrsz 3 car gar (almst 1ksqft), imm poss."*

Versus

4587 Queen Circle
> *"Total Remodel with a Twist! Loft Style! Exposed Brick! Exposed Ducts! New Hardwood Floors! New Maple Kitchen! New Granite Counters + Stainless Appliances! New Windows! Copper Gutters!"*

Send a copy of the listing to your seller. This is critical. Your seller needs to acknowledge that everything is correct and accurate to the best of his knowledge. This protects both of you. Don't fret when he wants to "improve" your written description or asks why you didn't mention the custom dog door. Explain, as above, that the MLS description is designed to attract buyers and agents to the door; once inside the home, they will be wowed by all the additional special features. If he insists on adding more detail, go ahead and do it. This is not a battle worth fighting.

Photography and Virtual Tours

Digital photos are a must in today's world. Many buyers shop online for homes and will skip over a home that doesn't have interior pictures. Buy a quality camera with a wide-angle lens and a flash and learn to take good interior pictures. If you don't want to invest in a camera, find a reliable photographer.

Virtual tours are not mandatory and if your seller doesn't request one, don't worry about it. A virtual tour (or lack thereof) probably won't affect the marketability of your listing. But if your seller wants one or you wish to include virtual tours in your listing services package, shop around for a good provider.

I do my own virtual tours through a company called Visual Tour (www.visualtour.com). Managing your own tours has many advantages, but if you prefer to hire an outside company to do them for you, make sure to schedule the tour right away.

SHOWING FEEDBACK

As soon as you've had your first showing, your sellers will be screaming for feedback! You need to have a system in place for obtaining the commentary from buyers and their agents.

There are three basic methods for obtaining feedback on showings.

The first is the good old-fashioned feedback request brigade - where agents call each other on Monday mornings, desperately seeking feedback for their anxious sellers. The script goes something like this:

"Hi, this is Jennifer Allan, I'm with Sell with Soul Real Estate. Thank you for showing my listing at 3065 Aspen Street on Saturday morning. To refresh your memory, it's the brick ranch with the bright red dining room, priced at $219,900. We'd love to hear your feedback on the property, and of course we'd love to see an offer! Please call me back with your thoughts. And thanks so much for showing our listing."

I estimate that I get a 25% response rate from telephone feedback requests.

The second way to obtain feedback is to fax a feedback request form with a list of standard questions to showing agents. Questions such as:

How did the property show? Good _____ Okay _____ Poor _____
How did you (and your client) feel about the price? Too High___
Just Right ___ Too Low _____

Is your client interested in the property? Yes _____ Maybe _____
No _____

Any additional comments? _____

I find that the faxed requests are almost always ignored.

The third method, e-mailing feedback requests, generates the best response in my experience. E-mail is quick and efficient for both parties (listing and showing agents) and also creates a paper trail (so to speak) that you can forward on to your seller.

Whichever method you choose, make sure to pass the feedback on to your sellers regularly, *especially during the first few days after the home goes on the market.*

Market Updates

I send written communication to my seller every three weeks or so. The first package goes out in the first week and includes the full MLS printout and a list of the current competition for their home, with photos. In this first package, I promise my sellers a market update in three weeks showing any new listings, price reductions, homes under contract and recent closings.

Subsequent market update packages include the recent market activity as well as the number of showings, virtual tour hits, Realtor.com hits and any other activity data I can track. Truthfully, most of my sellers never seem that interested in my market updates, but I send them anyway just to stay in touch.

After sending four market update packages, I usually ask my seller if she would like to continue receiving my updates. If she does, I keep sending them. If she says no, I do the updates on my own, just to keep up on the market in her neighborhood.

If, in the course of preparing your market updates, you see a new listing that is competing with your listing, you should preview it right away. It will make a Very Good impression on your seller if you call her to tell her all about the new listing on her block. If the new listing makes her listing look overpriced, well, you should share that information with her too (or at least offer to show it to her).

Samples of my market update letters are available on my website, www.sellwithsoul.com.

Staying in Touch with Your Seller

One of the most common complaints of home sellers is that they never hear from the listing agent after the sign goes in the yard. And frankly, if there's not much going on, it is easy to let time go by without contact. So I came up with several scheduled "topics" of discussion to give me an excuse to call my seller, even if I don't have much to report. For example, about a week into the listing, assuming we've had showings, I call my sellers to make sure the showing instructions are working for them or if they need to make adjustments. Other topics include my comments on any new competing listings I've previewed (see above), to check on their stash of flyers or to pass on feedback, of course. If my listing is vacant, I always call my seller after I go Fluffing & Flushing (see below) to report on the condition of the home. If there is anything he needs to address, or anything I corrected for him, I let him know.

Right after his home is listed, I send my seller an e-mail with all the links to the websites where his home is featured. I also include a link to the virtual tour and ask him to send the link out to his friends in hopes that someone will be interested. If nothing else, it's good advertising for me.

Six-Week Meeting with Seller

I tell my sellers up front that we will need to reevaluate the market about six weeks after we go on the market. Schedule an appointment with your sellers, prepare an updated CMA, review your feedback and show up with a plan and a smile.

Fluffing & Flushing

Fluffing & Flushing is the act of checking on a *vacant* listing during the listing period to ensure that everything is as it should be. And it never is. "Fluffing" refers to a general tidying up of the home (more below) and "Flushing" - well, have you noticed what happens to a toilet that hasn't been used in a while? Or worse - has been used but not flushed? Part of my service provided to my clients who own vacant homes is to flush their toilets for them!

If you have a vacant listing, you'll be dismayed how quickly things deteriorate into chaos. Shower curtains fall down, light bulbs burn out with incredible frequency, windows leak, lockboxes jam. Sure, it may be the sellers' responsibility to maintain the showing readiness of their home, but if the home is vacant they won't - and if you want it to sell, you'll probably need to do it yourself.*

If you find yourself with a lot of vacant listings, you'll want to pack a little crate for your car with the following items:

> Light bulbs
> Trash bags
> Dusting cloths
> Dirt Devil
> Windex and paper towels

* *If your listing will be vacant, ensure that your seller knows that it's his responsibility to maintain the home, and that even though you will commit to checking up on it periodically, it is his home. If a pipe bursts because the furnace failed, or the home is vandalized, you need to make darn sure your seller understands that he can't hold you liable, unless it's your fault, of course.*

The Colorado listing agreement addresses this issue by stating, "Neither Broker nor Brokerage Firm shall be responsible for maintenance of the Property nor shall they be liable for damage of any kind occurring to the Property, unless such damage shall be caused by their negligence or intentional misconduct." When I list a vacant home, I always point this out by saying, "Now, part of my service is to check on your home during the listing period and if I see anything amiss, I'll either fix it or let you know immediately. However, please remember that it's still your home and your responsibility to ensure that it is maintained. Be sure to keep your insurance current, and you might want to arrange for a friend to check on it for you as well."

I recommend checking on your vacant listings once a week. Here's what you're looking for:

Sign still up? Brochure box full? Lockbox operating smoothly? Porch light on? Yard need mowing? Watering? Snow being shoveled? Paper delivery canceled? Any strange smells in house? Power on? Heat on? Floor reasonably clean? Dead bugs? All doors locked? Windows secure? Toilets flushed? Garage door closed?

Gather up agent cards, flush the toilets, check the mailbox, make any corrections you can and make a note of conditions your seller needs to address. If nothing else, your weekly Fluff & Flush visits will give you something to talk to your seller about and show that you care!

A checklist for Fluffing & Flushing duties can be found on my website, www. sellwithsoul.com.

OPEN SUNDAY!

Most experienced real estate agents dread the Sunday Open House. But it's a necessary evil in our business and you might as well accept it. A good open house with a lot of traffic is actually a lot of fun, but a dead open house - ugh - is deadly. But even if it doesn't sell the home, there are several good reasons to hold an open house:

√   It makes your seller happy.

√   If the open house is active, you can get a concentrated dose of feedback from the general public.

√   Your open house may be the first time you've spent any real quality time in the home, so you may notice features or even potential problems that escaped your attention before.

√   And of course, the real reason agents hold open houses - the opportunity to prospect for buyers.

However, even during my first year when my prospecting antennae were way up and my enthusiasm and motivation were at their highest, I never got any quality leads from open houses. Oh yes, I got leads and prospects, but few, if any, closings. I'll stop short of saying open houses were a waste of time, though, because as I've stressed before, when you're learning the ropes, there's no substitute for being out there, even if you never get paid for it.

Selling Your Listing
Negotiating Offers

It's terribly exciting when you get offers on your first few listings. Well, actually, it's always exciting, even on your 90th listing.

When the offer(s) come in, your sellers will look to you for guidance. Hopefully.

Offers come in all shapes and sizes, with any combination of both attractive and deal-breaking provisions. Maybe the price is good, but the closing date is too far out. Or the price is low, but there's no inspection contingency. Rarely are offers everything you hope they'll be. Even in a multiple offer situation, there is often no clear winner - every offer has its quirks.

Here are the four most likely offer scenarios:

GOOD OFFERS

As you can imagine, these are the most fun and the easiest to negotiate. Obviously, a "good" offer is full price or close to, meets the seller's needs for timing and proposes reasonable dates and deadlines.

However, as the listing agent, I almost always look for something to counter in every offer. Even if the offer is close to perfect, I don't like to have my seller sign an offer as written. I have several reasons for this strategy.

First, I believe that if a buyer is going to have buyer's remorse, I'd rather get that over with up front. By countering the offer, even on a technicality, it gives the buyer an out if she is wavering. Some agents vehemently disagree with this strategy - they want that deal executed now. But since most contracts have inspection and loan contingencies, the buyer can easily terminate the contract after it is executed. And it's far more painful to terminate a deal than to never put it together in the first place.

Second, countering an offer keeps the balance of power ever so slightly tilted toward the seller (your client!). Yes, he is excited to receive such a fine offer on his house, but he's not desperate.

Third, when her offer is accepted as written, the buyer may wonder if she got her best deal. She begins to question herself, setting the stage for buyer's remorse. Maybe she should have offered less? By introducing a counterproposal, even if it isn't related to price, both buyer and seller feel the "thrill" of a successful negotiation.

LOW OFFERS

Everyone wants a deal. Many buyers want to try a lowball offer to see what happens. If your seller acts offended, go ahead and be offended with him. You'll win brownie points for being on his team. If you defend the low offer, he'll wonder if maybe you're in cahoots with the buyer's agent. Yes, sellers do think this way.

Once the seller has blown off a little steam (with your help!) and the annoyance is out of his system, you can begin to calmly discuss your counterproposal. Ensure that your seller is clear about the other provisions of the offer (besides price) such as the inspection period, the closing date, the date of possession and any requested seller-paid closing costs. Be sure to check your listing agreement ahead of time to refresh your memory on any exclusions! Point out the requested inclusions (e.g., refrigerator, washer, dryer, etc.) to the seller to make sure the buyer agent didn't sneak something in on you that your seller meant to exclude. I recently got to buy a washer and dryer for a seller because the buyer asked for them in the contract and the seller had specifically excluded them. And I forgot.

Your seller may want to counter at full price just to make a statement of his displeasure with the low offer. Try to get him to give a little bit (maybe a few thousand dollars) which will allow the buyer to accept without looking like a total putz. But if your seller is adamant, go ahead and cheerfully follow his direction. He is the boss!

What if your listing is overpriced and the low offer is reasonable? Well, hopefully your seller is aware that you think the price is high and that he pushed you to "give it a try." If that's the case, the best thing to do is to matter-of-factly remind the seller that buyer agents are looking at the same data you looked at when you gave your pricing recommendation. Period. Don't look smug or frustrated. Your seller isn't stupid and he needs to feel your support in order to make the right decision.

You'll put these deals together more often than you might think. Even a dismal offer can often be successfully negotiated.

MULTIPLE OFFERS

If you are in a market where multiple offers are common, your broker can probably better advise you on the local nuances of multiple-offer negotiation. Different states have different laws regarding the proper way to respond. I will tell you how I did it in Colorado, but be sure to check with your broker to make sure these strategies are legal and acceptable in your market.

√ Be sure that all buyer agents know that a bidding war is brewing. This can only help your seller get a higher price. Don't let anyone tell you that encouraging a bidding war is unethical. Nonsense!

√ If there is no clear winner among the offers (i.e., they are all strong), you can do one of two things:

1. You can notify all buyer agents that their buyer should present their best offer by a specific deadline (e.g., 6 p.m.). Tell them all offers will be presented at that time.

2. Counter all offers with an appropriate disclosure stating that there are multiple counterproposals in circulation (ask your broker for a sample).

Again, if you work in a market where bidding wars are common, check with your broker for other acceptable strategies.

Be aware that a bidding war may result in some conflicting emotions for both the seller and the winning buyer. The seller may feel an inflated sense of power over the buyer (and the market) and refuse to be reasonable during the inspection period and any subsequent negotiations. The buyer, on the other hand, may feel a little buyer's remorse after all the excitement and wonder if she got carried away in the bidding process. She may feel that the home better darn well be perfect and she may be overly fussy at the inspection.

CONTINGENT OFFERS

A contingent offer is one in which the buyer needs to sell a home to qualify to buy your listing. Here are three responses to a contingent offer:

1. Reject it, who needs the hassle?

2. Accept it, hopefully the buyer will be able to sell his home.

3. Counter with a First Right of Refusal.

Countering the offer with a First Right of Refusal means that the seller accepts the offer, but will continue to market the property. If the seller receives another acceptable offer, the seller notifies the first buyer that he must remove his home-sale contingency (and prove that he can close without selling his current home). If the buyer cannot or will not remove his contingency, then that contract is terminated and the seller is free to accept the second offer.

Contingent contracts are full of problems. Even if the contingent buyer is able to find a buyer for his home, the likelihood of your listing closing with this buyer is about half what it is with a typical non-contingent buyer. Think about it, instead of one potential deal-breaking inspection, there are two (the one on your listing and the one on the buyer's home). Instead of one loan approval contingency, there are two. Not one appraisal, two. Twice the opportunity for buyer's remorse or an unexpected job relocation.

So why would you ever accept a contingency? A few reasons:

√ **More money**

A good buyer agent knows that a contract contingent upon a home sale is not as appealing as a clean contract, therefore, the offer should be as attractive as possible in other respects. If you receive a contingent offer, you should expect a great price and reasonable terms.

√   **Market Realities**

As real estate prices move higher, first-time buyers are finding it harder to purchase a home. Therefore, the buyer for your listing may already be a homeowner who needs to sell his home to qualify to buy a new home.

In general, if your seller is committed to a specific moving date, it is probably a good idea to avoid contingent offers. Although, as discouraging as all this may sound, in my experience, most contingent deals do close. They're complicated and time-consuming, but if everyone can stay cool and flexible, there's a good chance of success!

Closing Your Listing

Incidentally, the seeds of this book were planted way back in my rookie year when I put my first listing under contract. I proudly marched into my office, with my executed contract and earnest money in hand ready to turn over to the office manager. She congratulated me and then asked which title company I was going to use. Huh?

Not wanting to appear clueless, I mumbled a non-answer and hurried away before she could push me for more details. I realized that I was experiencing one of those "you don't know what you don't know" moments. I surreptitiously asked the more experienced agents if I could borrow their "listing checklist" - y'know, the list they were given in real estate training to guide them through the contract-to-closing period? I must have missed that class because I never got mine. A Twilight Zone moment (for me). No one knew of such a list.

Some things I didn't know were my responsibility:

- Choosing the title company and ordering title work

- Preparing for and attending the appraisal

TITLE WORK

As used in this book, title work is the documentation provided by the title company showing current ownership of a property, along with any liens recorded against the property. In Colorado, "title work" also includes recorded HOA documents such as covenants and condominium declarations.

- Bringing the earnest money to closing

- Making sure all the disclosures are signed by the buyer

- Bringing the house key to the closing

- Taking down the sign and retrieving my lockbox and brochure box

Sure, I knew these things happened, I just didn't know who was supposed to make them happen...

Somehow I muddled through and got the house closed. I promised myself that I would create a checklist for myself with all the details that need to be handled as the listing agent during the contract-to-closing period. And thus - a checklist queen was born.

CHECKLIST FOR LISTINGS-UNDER-CONTRACT

This checklist addresses the items that are your responsibility during the period from contract-to-closing, as the listing agent. You can find the checklist without my commentary in the Appendix and on my website (www. sellwithsoul.com). It is formatted to be used as a check-off sheet for each listing if you aren't yet using a contract management program.

THINGS TO DO RIGHT AFTER CONTRACT IS EXECUTED

√   Get the earnest money check
If the offer and subsequent negotiations were handled via fax, don't forget to get the earnest money!

√   Turn in the executed contract to your office manager

√   Put contract dates in your contract manager program if you use one
Important dates include any objection deadlines (inspection, insurance, title, covenant review, appraisal, etc.), loan approval or any other agreements made in the contract. If you don't use a contract management program, enter these dates in your planner.

√   Order the title work (if it's your job to do so; each state is different)

√ Order HOA documents, if applicable

If your contract calls for the seller to provide recent HOA financial statements and/or meeting minutes, get these ordered right away if your seller doesn't have them (they never do). Some HOA managers now charge to provide this information, FYI.

√ Change the contract status in the MLS

√ Notify any agents with pending showings of the status change

√ Send the disclosures to the buyer's agent

√ Call the buyer's lender to introduce yourself

THINGS TO DO THE FIRST WEEK AFTER CONTRACT

√ Pick up the brochure box

√ Get payoff information from your seller

To pay off the seller's current loan, the title company will need the seller's social security number(s) and the seller's lender information (account number, customer service phone number). Don't forget to get this information for any second mortgages or home equity loans.

√ Has the buyer signed and returned the disclosures?

√ Put up SOLD sign

√ Call the buyer's lender to check on loan progress

THINGS TO DO TWO WEEKS AFTER CONTRACT

√ Prepare for the appraisal

As the listing agent, you should attend the appraisal with your sold comparables in hand, ready to defend the sales price if necessary. You should also have a printed list of all the upgrades and improvements to give the appraiser. Even if you have no reason to worry about the appraisal, it's a good idea to meet the appraiser at the property. It's professional and makes a good impression on your seller.

√   Set the closing
Notify all parties (seller, buyer agent, lender) of the time, date and location of closing.

THINGS TO DO DURING THE WEEK BEFORE CLOSING

√   Confirm that the inspection items are complete or scheduled

√   Confirm that the seller has arranged a move-out cleaning
More than once I have personally cleaned one of my listings because the seller didn't do it. It's embarrassing and awkward (and I'm a terrible maid). Now, I always ask my seller if she has arranged to have the home cleaned or if she needs me to arrange it. At least it puts her on notice that the buyer is expecting the home to be delivered in maid-clean condition.

√   Arrange a mail-out close or Power of Attorney (POA) if necessary
If your seller can't attend closing, make sure the title company knows ahead of time. They will send the closing package to the seller or prepare a POA for someone else to sign the closing documents.

√   Are there any changes that need to be communicated to the lender or title company?
Many times, contract provisions will be changed or renegotiated and no one remembers to let the lender and/or title company know. If you surprise the lender or title company with a material change at the last minute, your closing may be delayed, which makes everyone sad...

√   Is the buyer doing a walk-thru?
If so, let your seller know about it and leave the lockbox on the home. This is a good time to confirm with your seller that all the inspection items have been completed.

√   Confirm the closing date, time and location with all parties

THINGS TO DO RIGHT BEFORE CLOSING

√ Review the closing figures
Go over the figures with your seller to ensure there are no surprises at the closing table. If the seller's proceeds are different from the seller's expectations, now is the time to figure out why...not at the closing!

√ Order earnest money from your office manager, if applicable
Check with your office manager to see how earnest money escrows are handled. Protocol varies widely here. Just find out if there's something you are supposed to do.

√ Prepare the file for closing

√ Pick up the sign, lockbox and interior brochure box

AFTER CLOSING

√ Turn in the file to the office manager

√ Update your seller's address in your SOI manager

√ Call the seller a few days after move-out
Just thank him for his business and let him know you are always available for any post-closing questions or problems that may arise.

√ Add the seller to your post-closing follow-up plan

√ Update your website(s) with the sale

6

Negotiating Inspections
From both sides of the table...

Depending on your market, the Inspection Provision in your real estate transactions can cut your income in half - in other words, it's not unreasonable to see a lot of your sales fall apart over home repair issues, especially if you sell "charming" older homes. Inspections must be handled oh-so-carefully; the inspection period is full of land mines for the inexperienced agent. When you're good at negotiating inspections, you will feel an incredible sense of power over your income. I once had a run of 29 sales that successfully got through inspection to closing without one falling apart. In the "charming old Denver" market I specialized in, this was a significant achievement. And it felt goooooood. Successfully negotiating inspections is definitely a skill you'll want to excel at quickly!

Handling Inspections - As the Buyer's Agent

First, and hopefully obviously, always recommend that your buyer inspect the home to his satisfaction. Most trainers tell you to give your buyers a list of at least three general inspectors so that they can choose. Of course, the buyer may hire any inspector he likes outside of your list, or inspect the home himself if that's what he wants. But do advise him to hire a general inspector and encourage any other inspections that are typical in your market. In Denver, for example, I always recommend a sewer line inspection. If your buyer is concerned about radon, by all means tell him to have it checked out.

Don't ever, ever, ever talk your buyer out of an inspection; regardless of your intentions, it will be perceived as an attempt to save your paycheck. And, there might be some truth to that.

On my website there is a sample Inspection Information Sheet that I give to buyers during the inspection period.

Whether or not to attend the inspection is a topic of hot debate. Attorneys will tell you to avoid the physical inspection, or, if you must attend, "stand outside and smoke." Their point is that the inspection findings are between the buyer and his inspector and your presence there might somehow make you partially liable for the physical condition of the home.

I found this advice to sound good on paper (or in a GRI class), but impractical in practice. First, it's hard to negotiate repairs found during inspection that you didn't see firsthand. Second, your buyer expects you to be there and your credibility will take a little hit if you don't attend. Third, it's good customer service. Fourth, when you're new, inspections are an excellent opportunity to further your real estate education. Fifth, you need to be able to recommend good inspectors to your buyers and if you don't attend inspections, how can you judge? I don't see any way to avoid attending inspections without sacrificing the quality of your service to your buyer client.

The "Typical" Inspection

A "typical" inspection will reveal many minor maintenance concerns and often one major concern. A kitchen sink that leaks, a few improperly wired electrical outlets, a missing downspout, a slow-draining bathtub or asbestos-wrapped ductwork are usually easy fixes. Major concerns might be a damaged roof, a broken sewer line, an inoperable or dangerous heating system, structural stress or damage, or an outdated electrical system.

Handled correctly, these "typical" inspections can almost always be successfully negotiated. Even if your buyer's laundry list of minor items is three pages long and he insists on asking the seller to repair each and every one, you can usually hold this deal together.

DRAFTING THE INSPECTION REQUEST
FOR A "TYPICAL" INSPECTION

The goal is to create a punch list or inspection request list for the seller that doesn't feel abusive or punitive. We want the seller to agree to as many items as possible, without much back and forth negotiation.

Go through the inspection report with your buyer and identify the items he feels strongly about. Group the concerns into categories such as Plumbing, Electrical, HVAC, etc. If there is a major issue (e.g., the roof or furnace needs replacement), this is the first item on your request. Always ask that the major repairs be corrected by a licensed contractor with any required permits pulled and signed off on by the city inspector prior to closing.

Follow up with the other items, with as few bullets points as possible. If you have five plumbing issues, ask for all of them under one bullet. The four electrical issues get one bullet. A long punch list will put the seller (and the listing agent) in a bad mood before they even read it. I once got a two-page inspection notice that was made up mostly of requests for information, such as "Seller to identify the location of the main water shut-off" and "Seller to provide all instruction manuals and warranties to buyer at closing." The buyer only asked for three reasonable repairs, but my seller was so put off by the long "list," she initially balked at even doing those!

Make it easy for the seller to say "yes." Draft your request respectfully and do not imply by the words you choose that the home is in shameful disrepair. Simply state your requests and do not embellish them. For example, do not say, "Seller shall repair the leak under the kitchen sink to avoid further mold and mildew damage to the cabinet, flooring and possibly the basement ceiling." Simply say, "Seller shall repair the leak under the kitchen sink."

THE "INSPECTION FROM HELL"

Let's play a different game now. Let's pretend we're at a grueling four-hour inspection. Hail damage on the roof, a suspicious crack in the furnace, some structural cracks above windows and doors, evidence of termite damage - and we're just getting started. Stay calm. Watch your buyer's reaction. If he's upset, don't talk him out of it. Assure him that he doesn't have to buy the house if the physical condition is unsatisfactory to him, but that you will do your best to negotiate the repairs if that's what he wants. Whatever you do, don't belittle his concerns; he'll just dig in his heels. Your unconditional support will allow him to evaluate the situation objectively and make the right decision for himself without worrying about your disapproval.

If you have never gone through a difficult inspection before, this may all seem obvious to you, as a soulful real estate agent. Of course you will always support your client's wishes, right? Yes, in an ideal world, you would and you should. But, let's be honest, the world of commissioned sales is far from that utopia. When your commission check is on the line and you're watching your first (or second or third or tenth) sale evaporate before your eyes, you might find yourself doing things your soul would not approve of. It's human nature and I won't pretend that I never did it. I know that I pushed some buyers through a rough inspection out of my own desperation for a closing. It almost always came back to haunt me.

DRAFTING THE INSPECTION REQUEST
FOR AN "INSPECTION FROM HELL"

If the home truly is in surprising disrepair (i.e., the buyers weren't intending to buy a fix-up), go ahead and ask the seller to fix everything if that's what your buyers want you to do. Group your objections into categories and keep the language short and simple, not emotional or inflammatory. Include your inspection report if you think further explanation or clarification will be needed. Put some thought into the wording of your objections - don't just copy the inspection report word for word. This gives you, and your request, a little bit more credibility.

Don't be hostile with the listing agent. She wants a closing just as badly as you do and will be your greatest ally if she feels you and your buyers are behaving respectfully.

Keep in mind that the seller wants, and hopefully needs to sell her house. If she doesn't fix the problems for your buyer, she'll likely have to fix them for the next. Unfortunately, sometimes it takes a seller a few crashed deals to accept reality and it may be the next buyer who benefits from your buyer's experience. But if the seller is motivated and the listing agent is in control of her client, these deals can be salvaged if both parties want it to be.

HANDLING INSPECTIONS...AS THE LISTING/SELLER'S AGENT

As the listing agent, your primary job is to keep your seller calm during the inspection process. You'll also help him determine the best response to the buyer's demands, one that feels fair to him (or nearly so), yet satisfies the buyer. You may have to help him obtain bids and/or coordinate repairs.

A new listing agent can feel helpless when presented with a laundry list of inspection requests. Typically, she gives it to her client (the home seller), asks what the client would like to do, and passively delivers the response to the buyer's agent. Either the response is acceptable or it's not, either way, the seller's agent (you) did not take control and "solve the problem."

JENNIFER'S $0.02...

Subtly ask your seller to vacate the home during the inspection. The buyers need to start mentally taking possession of the home and this can't happen if the seller is hovering over them. Inspections are stressful, and the fewer personalities in the mix, the better.

Remember, sellers hire you to sell their house and get them to a closing. Believe it or not, they may not want to discuss or have an opinion on every single issue. If you appear to be in control of the situation, they will usually take your advice.

Of course, you need to know what to advise - especially during the inspection period. Every inspection negotiation is unique. Some sellers are sympathetic to the emotions and fears of the homebuyer; some think their home is perfect and are insulted by any insinuations to the contrary. Some have discretionary funds to make laundry list repairs; some are wondering if they will have enough equity to come to closing without their checkbook. I'll address each scenario below.

THE PERFECT SELLER

This seller understands that his home isn't perfect and that agreeing to reasonable inspection requests is just a part of the home-selling process. He is probably rather handy and is happy (well, not unhappy) to make most of repairs requested by the buyer. Even silly ones. You will have sellers like this, but as you can expect, not often. It's usually cheaper for the handy seller to make the nickel-and-dime repairs than for him to negotiate a credit with the buyer, so that's what I usually encourage him to do.

The Easily Offended Seller

This seller doesn't want to fix anything. She has been difficult since Day One, and might not want your advice anyway. She'll make comments like, "It was like that when we bought the house" or "There's nothing wrong with the furnace, it works fine," even though the inspector's report indicates a major carbon monoxide leak. When you are working with these sellers, here are a few strategies to get you past the inspection period.

Try to negotiate a dollar amount your seller is willing to spend toward repairs in the original contract. For example, you could state in your counterproposal, "Seller shall pay no more than $500 toward inspection items. This puts the buyer on notice that the seller will not be nickel and dime'd and, while it's not fool-proof, it works more often than you would expect. Some states already incorporate this wording into their contracts; perhaps yours does.

Sometimes if you say to your seller, "When you buy your next home, will you expect the major systems to be in good working order and if they aren't, will you expect the seller to fix them?" This works especially well if you will also be the buyer agent for the seller's replacement home. Or (very casually), "If I were the buyer's agent, I probably would ask for these items too."

On the other hand, remember whom you represent. If your seller does not want to fix anything and she thinks she is being reasonable, make your case once and then shut up. For two reasons. First, you never know, the buyer might just back down and accept the home "as-is" and if you tried to pressure your seller into doing more (and lost), you will look Very Bad in your seller's eyes. She will think you were trying to spend her money in order to secure your commission. Second, if the deal crashes over the inspection, the seller has a bigger problem than you do (you hope). Yes, I realize you just watched your paycheck vanish before your eyes, but hopefully your seller learned that, One) you do know what you're talking about, and Two) maybe she ought to look into the price of replacing that 60-year-old furnace she is so proud of.

I have worked with sellers who were so unreasonable at inspection that I had to terminate the listing because they clearly did not have a strong enough need to sell their home. But not often.

The Cash-Poor Seller

If your seller has equity in his home, but no cash on hand, inspection issues can be easily solved. You have two options. The safest thing to do in this situation is to negotiate a credit for the repairs that is paid at closing so that the buyer can make the repairs himself afterward. This credit will be taken from the seller's proceeds. If the buyer insists that the seller complete the repairs prior to closing, try to schedule the repairs as close to the closing date as possible so that the chances of buyer default are minimal. Arrange for the contractors to be paid at closing, again, out of the proceeds of the sale. Of course, if the sale unexpectedly fails, the seller will be liable for the repairs and you need to ensure he understands this risk.

If your seller has neither the funds nor the equity to make repairs, he simply may not be able to sell his home at this time. His needs and desires are irrelevant to the needs and desires of the market and he shouldn't expect a buyer to be sympathetic to his financial troubles. If the needed repairs are relatively minor and/or cosmetic, you might be able to persuade the buyer (or their agent) to accept the home "as-is," but a good buyer agent will negotiate a lower sales price. So your seller still loses.

* * *

A smart listing agent points out areas of concern (older furnace, worn roof, cracked windows, etc.) to the seller prior to listing. Don't dwell on these issues, just comment on them and gauge the seller's response. If he argues vehemently with you (and most will), just smile sweetly and say something like "Okay, no problem," then move on to other topics. And know that inspection will likely be a struggle.

On the other hand, don't be afraid to advise your seller to say "no" to the buyer's requests if they are truly unreasonable. But if your seller wants to sell and the buyer wants to buy, even difficult inspections can usually be successfully negotiated.

Whether you represent a buyer or a seller, your inspection negotiations will be far less painful and much more successful if you know what common repairs cost. The buyer's inspector will point out many deficiencies that will sound scary to an un-handy-man or woman. Buyers will panic over electrical and plumbing issues, even though most of them can be repaired for under $100. However, most buyers, sellers and even real estate agents assume any electrical work will run in the thousands. If you, as a buyer or seller agent, can speak with confidence about home repairs it will go a long way toward keeping your deals together.

Start familiarizing yourself with the costs of the following repairs/ improvements:

* Water heater replacement
* Furnace replacement (furnace less than 20 years old)
* Furnace replacement (furnace older than 20 years)
* Sewer line clean out
* Mid-grade carpet replacement (per square yard)
* Hardwood floor installation (price per foot)
* Hardwood floor refinishing (price per foot)
* Roof replacement (will vary widely)
* Gas fireplace conversion (from wood)
* Radon mitigation

Ask your broker for other repairs common in your market.

7

Serving Your Client, Not Your Paycheck
Adventures in Agency &
the Open Checkbook Policy

Adventures in Agency

Probably one of the first classes you took in real estate school was about agency. Whom you represent and how you represent them in a real estate transaction. This seemingly simple concept can generate hours of debate, even in advanced real estate classrooms. In every GRI class I took, we always spent at least an hour discussing agency issues, even in classes that had nothing to do with client representation.

Even experienced agents can forget the nature of their agency obligations. When you represent a client as his agent, you are obligated to look after his best interests and enabled to act on his behalf. Other interests shouldn't intrude - not yours, not the cooperating agent's, not the other party's (buyer or seller). In our enthusiastic negotiation, sometimes we lose sight of the party we are hired to protect, advise and be an advocate for. It happens.

This chapter is not meant to be a refresher course on the finer points of your market's agency laws and practices, or even an overview of the topic. You can find plenty of basic and continuing education opportunities to learn about agency and disclosure requirements, and it's a good idea to take one of these classes every so often - especially if you find yourself getting a little lax (it happens to all of us) in your own real estate practice.

Always keep your client's interests in the forefront of your mind and you won't go wrong. It's not always easy to do, because, believe me, even the most docile buyers or sellers are suspicious of you and *will* notice if you appear to place someone else's interests above theirs. Even if you are innocent, our profession has enough trust issues with the public; try not to add more. Just make sure you always strive to CYA by remembering who you are legally obligated to represent. (Hint, it's never you.)

Agency and Multiple Offers

Early in my career which was during the Denver real estate boom, I put a 1923 Bungalow on the market on a Monday morning. The home had been renovated and professionally staged. At 6:00 p.m. I had one offer on the home. It was not a perfect offer - it was not full price and was contingent upon the sale of the buyer's home. By 9:00 p.m., I had three phone calls from other agents telling me they were also bringing me offers. I let these three agents know that there was an offer on the table, and that it appeared a bidding war was brewing.

My seller was pleased with these developments (this is not always the case if it occurs to your seller that you might have underpriced his home). He instructed me to gather all offers and to do whatever I needed to do to elicit the best offer from each. We scheduled a time to meet the following evening to review all the offers.

Meanwhile, the agent for offer #1 was getting annoyed with me. He accused me of generating a bidding war (uh, yeah), and eventually threatened me with a complaint to the local Board of Realtors®. As I recall, the term he used was "ethical midget." Being rather new in the business, I was intimidated by his antics and immediately questioned myself - was I violating some unwritten code of conduct between real estate agents? (To clarify, in Colorado, there is no "first come - first served" rule when offers are made. Sellers do not have to respond to offers in the order they come in - they may pick and choose among all presented and respond to whichever one appeals to them. Your state may have different requirements).

We did indeed receive four offers on the home, one of which my seller accepted as written. It was an over-full-price, non-contingent offer with a three-week closing. The troublesome agent for the first offer harassed me for a week or so, but to my knowledge never took it any further. But his contention that I was unethical for encouraging a bidding war was way off base. My job was not to help *him* make his buyer happy, unfortunately. It's too bad that his buyer didn't win, but she wasn't the highest bidder. My job was to get my client (the seller) the most money and best terms for his home. Which I did.

I took an ethics class once where the instructor came right out and said "Agents should always be on the lookout for opportunities to make allies among other agents." He used a multiple-offer situation, similar to the one above, to illustrate how we can "do the right thing" to our fellow real estate professionals and thus guarantee smoother transactions on future encounters with these other agents. His recommendation when a bidding war is looming is to always try to work with the first offer you receive to "honor" that buyer and agent. That the agent will always remember and appreciate that you nipped a bidding war in the bud, just for him. Helloooooooo? If you cost your seller $10,000 because you refuse to generate a bidding war, do you think your seller will be sympathetic to your need for Friends in the Business on your Future Deals?

AGENCY AND OPEN HOUSES

Open houses are an area of much confusion when it comes to agency representation. I'm sure you have been taught what a great prospecting opportunity an open house can be - entire classes are taught on how to pick up buyers and solicit neighbors for future listings. However, please don't ever lose sight of why you're there.

> **JENNIFER'S $0.02...**
> *Put yourself in the seller's shoes - she is excited about your open house and is imagining that you are enthusiastically marketing all the special features of her home - not hungrily trying to build your business.*

Your job is to sell *that* home. If a potential buyer visits your open house and announces that she already has a buyer agent (who is probably taking the day off), you still need to graciously market the home to her. Show her around, politely answer her questions and, if you sense real interest, don't fuss that you're "wasting your time" on someone who isn't going to become your client. Every once in a while, you might even get to write an offer for a represented buyer, if the buyer is anxious and can't wait for her agent to come back from vacation.

AGENCY AND REPRESENTED BUYERS

If you have a lot of listings, you will find yourself doing the work of buyer agents who are apparently too darn lazy to actually show homes to their buyers. I get at least one phone call a week from a buyer who has an agent, but doesn't want to "bother him" until he finds the house on his own. So, Mr. Buyer calls listing agents all over town instead. Yes, it's your job to show your listing to this guy. If you refuse to show your listing to represented buyers, you could get in trouble with your seller, who expects you to show his home to any qualified buyer who calls.

I had an $900,000 listing once. My biggest listing ever. My area of expertise at the time was in the $200,000 to $400,000 range, so this was a Big Deal to me. I was amazed how many potential buyers called me directly, bypassing their buyer agents because "they didn't want to bother him, he's so busy." Of course, the buyer agents would expect to be paid a hefty commission ($25,000!) if their buyers bought the home, but they were just so darn busy <sigh>.

So, I showed the home and showed the home and showed the home, mostly to represented buyers. It was my job and I didn't even complain too much about it. Many listing agents will refuse to show their listing to buyers who have agents, and this is just plain wrong. Like it or not, it is your job to market your listing to all interested buyers, which in my opinion, includes showing it to buyers who already have a buyer agent.

However, one buyer took it a step further and pushed me over my limit. I showed the home to him three times, and then he asked me to "draft up a contract" for his agent's review because his agent was getting ready to go on vacation and didn't have time. What would you do?

Unfortunately, I told the buyer to get his agent involved and earn his commission. And I got fired from the listing for it, rightly so. My job was to sell that house. It wasn't my seller's problem that the buyer's agent was lazy. The seller wanted a closing, and he didn't care how resentful I might be paying the other agent who did next to nothing. I should have continued to work with the buyer (with the proper disclosures of course), keeping his enthusiasm high, and increasing his commitment level. Unfortunately, when the buyer's agent finally showed up, he talked the buyer out of the home - and I got fired.

Even knowing the outcome, if I had it to do all over again, I'm not sure if I could have handled the situation any differently. Some scenarios don't have a black and white answer, and if you can't handle that, you are in the wrong business. Just realize that jerks are found in real estate, just as in any other business. Even by being technically correct, you will get burned, you will get fired, you will get, pardon my French, screwed. It's an unfortunate part of the game and you must accept it.

I came up with one semi-effective way to tactfully encourage buyers to "bother" their agents. When they tell me they have an agent, I ask them to contact their agent and let the agent know that I am showing the property to them. I tell the buyer it's because most buyer agents would much prefer to show their clients homes personally (one would hope), and get annoyed with listing agents who don't refer the buyer back to their buyer agent. Sometimes it works; most of the time, I just get to do the buyer agent's work for him. Ah, well, all in a day's work.

John and the Dangerous Furnace

During the first semester of my rookie year, I worked with a buyer named John. The inspection on John's house revealed a dangerous furnace, emitting high levels of carbon monoxide. Since the home was occupied by a family with three small children, I notified the listing agent right away and asked in my inspection notice that the furnace be evaluated and replaced if necessary. The listing agent said, and I quote, "There's nothing wrong with that furnace and I would be happy to put that in writing for you! I should have known better than to accept an offer from a new agent, you obviously don't know what you're doing." Huh?

But apparently he relayed the information to his sellers, who had a slightly different approach. They had the furnace checked out and confirmed that it was indeed dangerous and that the family could wake up dead anytime. The listing agent called me up all chipper and cheerful with the news and casually asked me to call my buyer to see if he "wanted to pay half of the replacement cost of a new furnace."

Without analyzing the situation, I called up John and brought him up to date, including the seller's "offer" that John contribute to the replacement. John was quiet for a minute, then asked me innocently enough, "And why would I want to do that?" Duh. Why indeed? I stumbled around for an answer, couldn't find one. My inexperience led me to try to please the listing agent and seller instead of properly advising my client, the buyer. No harm done, except that I looked a little foolish; we refused to contribute toward the cost of the new furnace and moved on to closing.

You may be saying to yourself that you would never do something so brainless, and I hope you're right. But in the heat of negotiation, especially a contentious one, you might find yourself bending over backwards - in the wrong direction.

THE OPEN CHECKBOOK POLICY

When I was in real estate school, the instructor gave us a scenario that went something like this...

"You are in the heat of negotiations for a buyer client. You're close, but the buyer and seller are arguing over the possession of the refrigerator. It doesn't appear that either side is going to give and you're watching your paycheck vanish before your eyes over a crummy used appliance. The thought of hitting the streets again with this buyer makes your heart sink. Your buyer is not going to buy this home unless he gets a refrigerator - it's a matter of pride now. What do you do?"

We Licensees-in-Training were stumped. We threw out some suggestions; mostly along the lines of convincing either buyer or seller to change their mind. Nope, not what our instructor was looking for.

"You can buy the refrigerator" was his solution.

We were horrified. Not one of us had considered that possibility. Most of us came from traditional W2 employment situations and were not yet in tune with the realities of self-employment...i.e., you do what you gotta do to secure your paycheck. It was a huge AH-HA moment and 11 years later I still haven't forgotten it.

There will be times during your real estate career - and not just in the beginning - when opening your checkbook to make a problem go away is just good sense. Sometimes the problem at hand is actually your fault <gasp>. Sometimes it's just due to factors beyond your control and it may be the least painful way to get you to the closing. As you get more experienced and you learn to troubleshoot, hopefully these "opportunities" will present themselves less frequently. In the meantime, just consider these checks to be a cost of doing business and, more importantly, a learning experience. Tired of that phrase yet?

I'm the Proud Owner of a...Dead Tree!

My third sale ever - in November (this is relevant), my buyer client put a small home under contract on the east side of Denver. It was a rather stressful transaction, but it did close.

The following summer, my client called me, furious about a huge dead tree in his front yard. He insisted that the seller hadn't disclosed the existence of the dead tree, and it was going to cost him at least $1,000 to have it removed. I vaguely remembered seeing something about a "dead or diseased tree" in the Seller's Property Disclosure, and confidently went to the file to pull it out. "AH HA!" I exclaimed to myself - "Here it is!" And, indeed, there it was, plain as day - the sellers did disclose the existence of a dead tree. I was relieved that I wasn't going to have to make an issue about non-disclosure.

But...uh oh.

My buyer hadn't signed the disclosure. No initials, no signature, no evidence that he ever even saw it. So there I was - no proof that I had ever presented the Seller's Property Disclosure to my client.

I wrote my buyer a check for $1,000. I did it cheerfully, without argument. It was my fault - I was his buyer agent. Sure, it was a painful check to write during my business-building period, but I did it. And, you know what? He still refers people to me and still fondly remembers that I bought his dead tree. It's turned into a good story and bought me more good PR than all the feel-good mailers in the world could have.

Don't be too proud to take responsibility for your mistakes. You'll be surprised at the good press you will receive for your integrity.

Don't Make Me Put Priscilla Back in My Car!

Remember Priscilla? Well, I finally found Priscilla a home she was happy with and, after some painful negotiation, got it under contract for her. The next step was the inspection, which went surprisingly well. However, Priscilla had annoyed the seller so much during the negotiations to date that the seller refused to make any repairs to the home, even reasonable ones. Priscilla loves to beat up (sorry, negotiate with) the opposing party, so by God, the repairs were going to be made or she would walk away. Before it became a vicious standoff, I stepped in and paid for the repairs. I never told Priscilla about it because she wouldn't have accepted my money - she thought she had won the negotiation and she was happy.

The Square Footage that Didn't Count

My fix-n-flip clients, Barbie and Ken, purchased a crummy little house on a crummy little street - can you tell I was less than enthusiastic about their purchase? I hated the house and wasn't excited about the prospect of selling it for them down the line after they renovated it. I didn't think it was marketable and knew they would eventually blame me when the home didn't sell.

The home was an 1890 cracker box (sorry, single story home) with a finished attic. The attic area had sloping ceilings which made it usable only for children or small adults. The access stairs were steep and difficult.

Miracles do happen and we found a buyer for the home. All was going well until the appraisal. The appraiser refused to consider the attic space in his total square footage, due to the sloped ceilings and difficult stairway, and reduced the value of the home accordingly; I believe he appraised the home $10,000 lower than the sales price.

My sellers were furious...at me. It hadn't occurred to me that the attic space might be an appraisal problem, although I had certainly been concerned about it as a marketing challenge. Barbie and Ken claimed I should have warned them about a potential appraisal problem before they purchased the property and perhaps they were right. But regardless, my sellers were going to have to reduce their sales price by $10,000 if they wanted a closing. I (grudgingly this time) kicked in my entire commission on the home to help offset their loss.

Oops! The HOA Fees Went Up!

When you're working with condos and townhomes (see Chapter Eight), you need to be aware of a whole new set of issues. One of these is changing Home Owners Association (HOA) fees. HOA's can and do raise their fees. If you are listing a property with an HOA, you need to periodically check in with your seller or the HOA itself to confirm that the fee you are advertising is still correct. If your buyer is purchasing a property with an HOA, you or your buyer should call the HOA directly to confirm the fee.

I once represented a buyer in the purchase of a $50,000 condo. The condo had been on the market for six months and the HOA fee advertised in the listing material was $150/month. At the closing, we discovered that the fee was actually $175/month. Either the listing agent made a mistake or the fee had been increased during the term of the listing, but either way, my buyer wasn't happy at all.

Increasing the monthly payment on a $50,000 condo by $25 is a Big Deal to the buyer of a $50,000 condo. Not just out of principle; it was truly a financial burden for her. After an awkward pause, I offered to reimburse my buyer one year's worth of the difference (25 X 12 = $300). I fully expected the listing agent to kick in too since it was clearly his misadvertising, but he did not. Technically, as a buyer agent, it was probably my responsibility to protect my buyer, but I did feel that the listing agent could have shown a little soul and kicked in a couple of dollars.

Kathy's Stove

Even if you read this book cover to cover and have been selling real estate for 50 years, you will still come across situations that you couldn't have anticipated. The kind that will make you look like the bad guy if you don't fix them for your client. Which will often involve a check with your signature on it.

I sold a condo to my buyer, Kathy. Kathy was scraping her pennies together for the down payment and closing costs and didn't have much left over. During the inspection of the condo, we discovered that the stove didn't work and asked the seller to replace the stove with a comparable unit (thought I covered myself there!). The seller agreed and we proceeded toward closing.

The day of the final walk-thru just prior to closing, we discovered that the stove the seller purchased didn't fit into the space where the stove was supposed to go. It was too big (huh?)...apparently the stove that had been in the condo was the original stove put in by the builder and was a custom size (probably due to an expensive mistake by the kitchen designer). The replacement stove purchased by the seller protruded from the front of the cabinets about four inches, and blocked the dishwasher and a drawer from opening. Gee, I didn't think to put in my inspection notice that the stove should fit!

Kathy did some quick research and found that the price of a custom-sized stove was around $1,000 (a decent typical-sized stove should cost around $500). We asked the seller to replace the stove, but he refused. The listing agent also refused to contribute toward solving the problem. So, I opened my checkbook and split the cost of the new stove with Kathy. Was it my fault? No. Was it my problem? Absolutely.

> **CAUTION!**
> *Beware of homes with freshly renovated kitchens! The space allowed for appliances is not always standard, especially the space for the refrigerator. If the appliances are not installed or included, make sure your buyer measures the space to ensure that they will not have to purchase a custom (i.e., expensive) appliance.*

In Defense of the Open Checkbook Policy

In the above example of Kathy's Stove, how do you think Kathy would have felt about me, had I just shrugged my shoulders and let her absorb the cost of the new stove? Sure, she knew it wasn't my fault the stove didn't fit, but she still had every right to expect me to fix the problem for her. When the seller and listing agent refused to contribute to the cost of a replacement stove, I had two choices. I could continue to bully them by threatening to terminate the contract, or I could step up to the plate and help her buy the stove. (Or, of course, the third option, just shrug my shoulders and sheepishly walk away with my commission check.)

You might be saying to yourself "Well, that's because she's shy - she doesn't have the guts to fight it out," and I see your point. However, I don't consider a "lack of guts," used in this context to be such a bad thing. I like to sleep at night, and if I can avoid an avoidable confrontation, I'll do it in the interest of expediency and peace of mind. Were the seller and listing agent wrong? In my opinion, yes, they were dead wrong. Was I willing to risk all the good will I'd built up with Kathy by starting an ugly battle that I would likely lose? Apparently not.

But having soul isn't synonymous with being a pushover, so lest you believe that the Open Checkbook Policy somehow implies that I think soulful salespeople don't stick up for themselves, let me set you straight. Sure, it's soulful to care enough about your client to be willing to spend your "own" money to solve their problem, but it's also often in your best interest too. When you're crazy-busy, you need to choose which battles to fight and which battles to take the easy way out. If you can buy your way out of a problem instead of spending lots of hours and lots of energy, sometimes it's the wiser choice.

Another benefit of having your own Open Checkbook Policy is that it will help give you peace of mind in those times where you really need a closing. Many potential deal-breaking problems in a real estate transaction can be solved by throwing money at them. While it's not a habit you want to get into, it's good for you to know that if you have to, you can ensure yourself a closing by opening your checkbook.

You will run into these situations many times in your career. Each time, you will have a decision to make. Trust your gut - do what feels right to you. Legally, it's not your duty to take financial responsibility for others' mistakes, but every once in a while, it might just be the right thing to do.

137

8

Special Types of Sales
New Construction, Condominiums & FHA

Selling New Construction

As a buyer agent, you may be involved in helping your buyer client purchase a home from a builder. In most cases, this is easy money for you. It's easy unless the builder is a flake, but even then, it's probably less stressful than a traditional real estate transaction. You don't have a large role in the process and the "seller" (the builder) isn't nearly as emotional as a regular home seller can be.

Here are some answers to questions you may have about selling new homes:

Will the builder honor my relationship with my buyers if they look at the home without me present (this is, will I get paid?)

Don't fret, this happens all the time. Most new home builders have a policy that buyers must register their agent with the builder on their first visit to the site. You don't usually have to be with your buyers, but they must declare in writing that they have a buyer agent when they sign in at the model home. If they don't, and they subsequently purchase a home from the builder, the builder does not have to pay you a commission, regardless of any buyer agency agreement you may have with your buyer.

When (not if) you get a call from the buyer you've driven all over town telling you about the great new home he found, just call the sales office right away. Don't be afraid to make the call; on-site sales people have heard it a hundred times. They will almost always let you in on the deal. If they won't, well, you learned something. Real estate is a constant learning experience, in case you haven't noticed.

What is my role in the sales process?

You will be given a disclosure from the on-site salesperson explaining your duties as the buyer's representative. Usually you must attend the signing of the contract, the final walk-thru and the closing. The builder's representative handles everything else. You don't need to go to the design center with your buyer to pick out flooring, attend construction walk-thru's or meet with the buyer's lender.

Are the builder's prices negotiable?

In my experience, no. The market may change or vary by region, but unless you hear otherwise from your broker, don't feel that you need to earn your fee by negotiating the price. Builder contracts are rarely negotiable in any way. You'll just frustrate yourself and your buyer by asking for something the on-site sales person can't give you.

Should the buyer use the builder's lender?

Probably. If the home builder is a big company (not a small local builder), they may own a mortgage company and will offer incentives for your buyer to use their own lenders. These incentives can be substantial; I've seen incentives as high as $30,000. Your buyer can't turn that down and your own lenders can't compete, obviously. Even small builders usually have an independent preferred lender who will offer smaller incentives - perhaps a no-closing cost loan or a credit toward upgrades.

Another reason to use the builder's lender is that some builders are real sticklers when it comes to the closing date. If the buyer is using an outside lender and the lender makes a mistake and can't close on the specified date, the builder just might threaten the buyer with default. If the buyer is using the builder's lender, and he misses the closing date, the builder can't really say anything. The builder's lender is also familiar with the project - the HOA, the financials, the appraisals.

One caveat, though. More than once I have seen a builder's lender do a bait-n-switch with my buyer (this has only happened with the big corporate builders). Right before closing, the lender announces that, for some obscure reason, he can't do the loan he promised, and therefore the buyer must put down more money or accept a higher interest rate.

I've never quite figured out why this happens so consistently - I don't think that the lenders do it on purpose. My best guess is that builder's lenders are somewhat sheltered from the real world of lending and aren't as experienced at recognizing and heading off potential problems early on.

As the buyer's representative, the best you can do is warn your buyer ahead of time that there may be loan issues at the last minute. If he has a relationship with another lender, it might be a good idea to recommend that he have a backup plan in place in case the builder's lender refuses to do the loan all together. If this happens, sometimes the builder will honor the incentive even if the buyer uses an outside lender.

Should my buyer hire a professional inspector?

YES YES YES! I always insist that my new home buyers have their home inspected by an independent inspector. Inspectors are trained to go through a home and identify issues and items that need correction; your buyer is not. Just because the builder has a signed Certificate of Occupancy from the city building inspector does not mean that the dishwasher is hooked up properly, that the windows open and shut smoothly, or that the sink stoppers are installed. It is not at all uncommon for the inspector to find dozens of action items and it is far easier (and more convenient) to have these items corrected before the buyer closes and takes possession.

Should I take buyer agency?

I do not believe in accepting buyer agency in new construction; I prefer to be a transaction broker (neutral party) when working with a builder. Why? Because in most cases, the buyer will have a direct relationship with the builder, one in which I have no control. They will meet with the builder without me, and I don't want to take responsibility for the builder's work. Additionally, I do not write the contract and am not intimately familiar with it as I would be with the standard contracts prepared by the state.

* * *

Selling Condominiums

Condominium sales present a few wrinkles in the process that you don't find in the sale of single family homes. Following are some questions you should get answered when involved in the sale of a condo, whether you're the listing agent or the buyer representative.

√ **Is the building FHA-approved?**

Your lender should be able to answer this question for you. If the building is not approved by FHA, it is probably because the rental ratio is too high (i.e., too many rental units in the building compared to owner-occupied units), or the building was built or converted to condos too recently. As the listing agent, you need to know the status of FHA approval so you know whether to advertise FHA financing or to accept an FHA offer.

If you are working with an FHA condo buyer on the lower end of the market in your area, you need to be sure to only show the buyer FHA-approved condos. Keep in mind that the less expensive condo projects are likely to have high rental ratios and many may not be FHA eligible.

√ **Is there a "working capital" requirement at closing?**

I was burned once with this one. Many homeowner's associations require that buyers make a working capital deposit with the association at closing. This working capital requirement might be as much as three times the monthly HOA dues (e.g., if the monthly HOA fee is $175, the working capital due at closing would be $525). In Colorado, for instance, there is no mention of the working capital requirement in the standard contract so buyers are almost always caught by surprise the day before closing. If your buyer is counting pennies to come up with her down payment, this will be a nasty surprise. You, as the buyer's representative, might just get to pay the working capital deposit at the last minute to keep your closing together. If you are the listing agent of a condo, it's a good thing to know about; if the working capital deposit is more than a few hundred dollars, you might want to make the other agent aware of it up front to avoid last minute hassles.

How was I burned? I sold a $150,000 condo that had an $825 working capital deposit requirement that I wasn't aware of. The buyer's father felt that I, as the buyer's agent, should have told them about the requirement at the time they wrote the offer. I paid the $825.

√ **Are there pet restrictions?**
Some high-rise buildings do not allow pets or impose limits on size.

√ **Are there any move-in/move-out procedures?**
Some high-rise buildings require notice for move-in/move-outs. They may not allow moves over the weekend and may require a damage deposit (sometimes non-refundable).

√ **Confirm the HOA fees and what they cover!**
Whether you represent the seller of a condominium or a buyer purchasing one, always call the association and confirm what the monthly/quarterly fees are and what exactly they cover. If you have a property listed for a long period of time, you need to periodically reconfirm the fees. If you are advertising the wrong amount, you could be liable for paying the difference, or even killing the sale if the buyer is at the top of his price range already. If your buyer gets to the closing table and finds out the fees have recently been raised, he may understandably get testy. And who do you think he is annoyed with....? It gets ugly and everyone looks bad - well, the real estate agents do anyway.

✳ ✳ ✳

As you may suspect, I created condominium checklists for my condominium buyers and sellers. They can be found in the Appendix and on my website, www.sellwithsoul.com. The first is the list of questions I use for myself when listing a condominium - I call the association and ask my questions, taking notes.

The second is a list of questions I use when I am representing a buyer; I usually call and ask the questions on behalf of my buyer, although I advise my buyer to do the same. In fact, I don't tell my buyers that I intend to make the call because I want to give them the responsibility for communicating with the HOA. Of course, if the HOA tells me something critical my buyers need to know, I will pass on that information, but in general, I give them the impression that verifying HOA information is up to them.

I learned this early in my career after I dutifully called an association president and was told that maybe, probably not, but perhaps there might be an assessment for new windows in the distant future. Right or wrong, I did not pass on this information to my buyer (probably wrong). Of course, within six months the association approved a $1,000 window replacement assessment and my buyer was furious with me. He felt that I had purposely withheld the information from him in order to secure my commission. That's hard to argue against and may have had some truth to it. Ouch. Like I said earlier, it happens.

* * *

FHA Loans

If you work in a metropolitan area, you will deal with FHA loans. And you will hate them. But unless you enjoy helplessly watching your deals fall apart at the last minute, you better know your enemy well.

While there are many troublesome nuances in an FHA loan, most problems arise in the appraisal. Which, unfortunately, means they come up later rather than sooner, since appraisals aren't usually done until late in the transaction.

While a conventional appraisal is simply a justification of value, an FHA appraisal goes much deeper. The appraiser must verify that the home is in good condition according to government standards. If the property does not meet these standards, the conditions must be corrected prior to closing.

Common red flags include peeling paint (a lead-based paint hazard), broken windows and missing hand railings. Any obvious structural condition (cracks in walls, sloping floors) will almost always kill your deal. The electrical system must be updated (no fuse boxes) and an older furnace must be certified. A rough-looking roof will be tagged, and all flat roofs must be inspected and certified by a roofer. Remember, all this is happening a week or so before closing! And, repairs must be made before closing - FHA rarely allows a repair escrow unless it's a weather-dependent item like a new roof.

Minor issues can usually be corrected in time. However, a seller might be understandably reluctant to make additional FHA-required repairs to a home after he has already negotiated the inspection. Many times, the *buyer* will spend his Saturday painting a home he doesn't own in order to get his loan approved. I once had to tell my seller that he had to replace the worn-out roof on a rickety lean-to porch to satisfy FHA. The worst part? The buyer was going to tear off the porch right after closing!

You need to be able to recognize potential problems long before the appraisal. If you are working with a fix-up buyer, try to dissuade him from using FHA financing. Warn your buyer that he may get to paint a house he doesn't own (in January) or pay for minor repairs (window replacement, hand railings) before closing. Sellers will usually do it, but be prepared for ones who won't.

If you are listing a house with an obvious FHA concern such as a questionable roof, furnace or electrical system, don't advertise that you will accept FHA financing unless your seller is willing to make the repairs or replacement. In my opinion (and I am not an attorney), offering FHA, implies that the seller will comply with the FHA requirements, even after negotiating any inspection items. Whenever I can get away with it, I add a provision in my counterproposals stating, "By accepting FHA financing, Seller is not agreeing to make any repairs required by an FHA appraisal." Sometimes the lender makes me take it out, but I always try.

The reason I say that a structural problem will almost always kill an FHA deal is because the appraiser will require a "Structural Certification" from a structural engineer. Now, in my experience, no structural engineer is going to "certify" a home that has some structural problem significant enough to be noticed by an appraiser. He will always require that some work be done by a licensed structural contractor and it won't be cheap or quick. It can be done

- I once got some structural work completed in a week on a home that was almost in foreclosure, but I had a highly motivated seller.

Some excellent reading on FHA appraisal requirements can be found at www. FHAinfo.com. Seriously, it's good reading.

BE AWARE OF TWO OTHER FHA ISSUES:

√   **"Disallowable" Loan Fees**

There are certain loan closing costs that the buyer is not allowed to pay. Traditionally, the seller pays these costs, but he isn't required to. If the costs are reasonable - say up to $250 or $300, it usually isn't a problem. But some lenders charge much more and the seller doesn't find out about it until closing. Surprise! The seller's settlement statement shows $800 in buyer loan fees! Again, the seller is not required to pay these fees, but if he wants to have a closing, he'll pay them. But he won't be happy and if you are the listing agent, you'll get some of the blame. You might even get to pay the fees yourself (and add it to your "learning experience" list).

You can head off this problem by stating in your counterproposal that the seller will pay "no more than $xxx toward buyer's loan costs." If the fees are higher than that, everyone has been warned. The lender can absorb the fees or the buyer's agent can kick in.

√   **FHA-Approved Condominiums**

Not all condominiums are eligible for FHA financing. New projects rarely are, nor are buildings with high non-owner occupancy ratios. If you are working with an FHA buyer in a lower price range, you may have trouble finding FHA-approved condos. Just be aware. You can find out the FHA approval status of a condo by asking your lender.

9

So You Want to Be a Licensed Assistant?
The Realities of "Easing into Real Estate"

If you live in an area where real estate is not booming, you may have considered becoming a licensed assistant for an established agent. Just for a while, you tell yourself, so you can learn the business without the risk. In a year or two, you'll go out on your own. I get a couple of calls a month from new licensees wondering if I'd be interested in hiring them as a buyer agent or licensed assistant.

Quite frankly, no, I'm not. Interested that is. But more on why that's so a little later.

Be warned, if you're brand new, I'm going to try to talk you out of going the licensed assistant route at this point in your career. It doesn't make sense for you or the broker you would work for.

A licensed assistant works under an active salesperson. Activities range from clerical inbox duties to working independently as a buyer agent. With the right combination of skills and personalities, a salesperson / licensed assistant team can be wildly successful. The wrong combination will be a waste of everyone's time, money, energy and emotion.

WHO MAKES A GOOD LICENSED ASSISTANT?

I, for example, have the skills (although not the personality) to be a great licensed assistant. A licensed assistant must be detail-oriented and enjoy paperwork. Not tolerate it, but actually enjoy it. She must be computer-literate. She must be reliable and organized. Happy to play behind the scenes. Not interested in the limelight. Not interested in building her own business. In other words, a licensed assistant is everything a top salesperson typically is not. Well, duh - that's why the top salesperson needs her.

Therefore, why do you think you'd be a better licensed assistant than you would a full-time agent? Assuming you went to real estate school hoping to be a Top Dog someday, do you really think you have the personality to be the opposite: a behind-the-scenes assistant? You're probably way more extroverted than I am and it would be hard for shy little me to give up control of my career and my income to be an assistant. It's just not in the makeup of a successful real estate agent.

If you're thinking, "Yeah, I can do it, for now," just beware that you may never break out of the assistant role. It can get pretty comfortable and a great licensed assistant can make good money. If you aren't willing or able to take the plunge into selling real estate now, what makes you think next year will be any different?

I guess what I'm trying to say is that if you think you'll be a great licensed assistant, you'll probably never be a great (or happy) real estate agent. And vice versa. Sorry.

BUT IT GETS WORSE...

As a brand new licensee, you don't have much to offer a high producing salesperson. You don't know the systems, you may not know the market, you don't have any experience preparing contracts, CMA's, brochures or other marketing material. You've never held an open house. You've never set showings. You don't know how to order title work. You need to be trained in every single aspect of your job. A Top Dog doesn't have the time or patience for that. And to actually pay you for the privilege of teaching you how to do your job? That goes against everything a top producing real estate agent believes in. Especially (and this is critical) if you've made it clear you intend to go out on your own someday. Why, oh why would a successful real estate agent take his time to train you, share his secrets and client list with you, even share his paycheck, knowing your goal is to be his competition someday?

Therefore, an ideal licensed assistant is an experienced agent who definitely no longer wants to sell. Perhaps she was never as successful as she dreamed she'd be, or she realized that she's not cut out for the stress of a full-time real estate agent's life. She's had her fun, now she's happy to play a support role.

If You're Bound and Determined...

So you still want to try this assistant gig? Okay, I'm happy to help. First, take a little time and get some training. If you're brand new and don't know how to work your local MLS, take a class or pay another agent to teach you. Make sure you know a desktop publishing program or two (e.g., Microsoft Publisher). Visit open houses and observe how the agents behave. Take a contracts class offered by the local board of Realtors®. Learn Top Producer or another contact management program. Know how to take and process digital photos. Read books about real estate. *The Complete Idiot's Guide to Success as a Real Estate Agent* is a good one. In other words, don't expect a successful real estate agent to train you in the basic functions of your job. Take the initiative to learn this stuff yourself.

I, for one, would be very impressed with you if you approached me with this can-do attitude, even if you were brand new.

Finding a broker to work for is likely a matter of networking. Successful real estate agents are too busy to make a concerted effort to find help. You will probably have to pretty much show up under her nose with a plan and a smile. Most overwhelmed agents I know all say they'd love to hire an assistant, but they just can't seem to get around to it. You might try making an appointment with the managing brokers of a few offices; they might know if there is someone in the office who would be interested in your services.

I'll tell you what *will* increase your street appeal to a potential broker/employer - if you have a large circle of friends you'd be willing to share with him and let him add to his SOI - now that's worth something. However, if you intend to set off on your own in a few years, this is obviously a bad idea. If you're not willing to let your broker prospect to your SOI, just be sure to negotiate a referral fee if you bring in business yourself.

Real estate agents are notoriously cheap. So unless you really have something special to offer an agent, don't expect much in the way of compensation at first. As a new licensee, you have a lot to prove to a Top Dog or Top Dog Wannabe before they're going to be willing to make much of a financial commitment to you. If you're willing to work on commission only, you can probably negotiate a better deal for yourself. If you want a guaranteed salary, you will probably be offered an hourly rate just slightly higher than what the office receptionist makes. I hired an assistant once and paid her $12/hour, which was considered quite generous. And she had experience.

Again, if you're satisfied with $12/hour (just for now, of course), you may not be cut out for a career as a real estate agent. And that's okay!

Being a licensed assistant is an honorable career in itself, not a logical stepping stone between real estate school and a true real estate career. Because the skills, interests and personalities required to succeed are so different between the two jobs, it just doesn't make sense. If you want to sell real estate, go sell real estate. You can do it, I promise.

10

Some Final Thoughts, A Few More Stories & Last-Minute Advice

Don't Get Too Caught-up in One Prospect

When you're a new agent, you tend to see everyone you meet as prey. If they have a real estate need, you're determined to be the one to meet it and you'll take it personally if they don't use you. Try to keep things in perspective and don't get too upset if someone you know uses another agent, or otherwise "cuts you out of the deal." If you behave badly, you will be embarrassed years down the road at your lack of sensitivity to your prospect's situation and needs. I hope you are, anyway.

Brian was one of my biggest investor clients and my main source of referrals in my early years. In my second year of business, Brian bought a townhouse (using me as his buyer agent) as a fix-n-flip investment. Of course, I was counting on listing the townhouse when the renovation was completed, and since I was relatively new to real estate, this was a Big Deal to me.

Well, one thing you'll have to get used to if you work with investors is that they are hoping for a profit (duh) - the bigger the better. If they can eliminate real estate fees, which are a huge cost of doing business for an investor, they'll quickly cut you out of the deal. During renovation, their project may attract a lot of unwanted (in your opinion) attention from buyers and real estate agents. Unfortunately, you can't stand guard on "your" listing 24 hours a day to protect it from intruders. Your investor might get cocky (you admit it) and figure he doesn't need you.

Brian did end up selling the renovated townhouse himself, to a walked in off the street. He didn't have to pay anyone a commission, saving himself around $9,000. I was heartbroken and for a moment considered terminating our professional relationship.

Is this tacky or what? Luckily, I handled it professionally (sheer willpower on my part) and our relationship continued. Always, when a client does something that takes money out of your pocket, try to see the situation through his eyes before you react. What he did was probably reasonable, and besides, it's done now...move on.

Here's another story. During my first year in real estate, a work associate from my past life listed her home for sale...with another agent who happened to be the dominant agent in the neighborhood. I was, again, heartbroken. Her explanation to me was that she didn't want to hire a "friend" (a tactic you'll encounter throughout your career; many times it will work for you when a "stranger" prospect hires you instead of their best friend). In retrospect, I'm sure she didn't want to hire a brand new agent, and I can't blame her. But I got mad and wasted lots of emotional energy being mad. Get used to it. Be grateful for all the friends who do hire you, even though they know perfectly well you probably aren't the most qualified. Soon enough you will be able to convince your friends to hire you not just because they like you, but because you're an extraordinary real estate agent.

When you get blown off or cut out, go ahead and be heartbroken for an hour or two. If you really want to, you can lose a night's sleep over it. Sure, you might have wasted some time, you may be counting on the commission to pay your mortgage (you know better though, don't you?), but these things happen. It's a tradeoff...sometimes deals fall into your lap with little effort on your part. Don't destroy a friendship and/or your credibility by pouting or fussing. It gives real estate agents a bad name, and certainly reduces your chance of getting referrals from this person. Graciously accept defeat, and offer to help if you can. After all, you would probably have done the same thing in a similar situation. Remember that.

Play Fair with Referrals

In a desperate quest for a paycheck, new real estate agents sometimes do things that are embarrassingly self-serving. We all did them and you will too. Things that later in your career make you cringe (I hope).

When I was new in the business, I found myself frantically pursuing referral fees. Just because I was now "In Real Estate," I felt entitled to collect money from the agents who already had relationships with friends and family members. My older sister was a real estate investor in California who regularly purchased high-dollar properties. I actually approached her to see if she thought her agent would mind paying me referral fees on my sister's deals. Is that tacky or what? But not that unusual.

Throughout your career you will pay referral fees to other agents who did nothing to earn them, most commonly a relative in another state who happens to have a real estate license. Even if you found your client all on your own, even if she's your best friend, you'll be asked to pay a referral fee. It's your call. As a new agent, you will probably just shrug your shoulders and be grateful to have any business at all. Later you might be willing to take a stand or let the prospect go. Just hope that all the referring party wants is a piece of the financial action and not to "help out."

Some of the most miserable deals I've ever had were representing buyers whose mothers were real estate agents. Nothing you do is good enough, you can't negotiate hard enough, your contracts will never be written strong enough. She will second-guess every move you make and fill her precious darling's head with all kinds of nonsense that you'll somehow have to tactfully deprogram. It's a nightmare.

Anyway, back to referrals. Don't ask for referral fees you didn't earn. It's beneath you. Also, if you're going to refer your client to another agent, please do a little homework and make sure it's a reasonable match. Make a phone call or two. Don't just open your handy-dandy Re/Max Referral Catalog and give out a phone number - a little pre-screening will go a long way toward ensuring a satisfied client and thus an eventual referral check in your pocket.

With regard to referrals, I ask for (and pay out) 20% for listings and 25% for buyers. I feel that since listings typically cost the listing agent money out of pocket, it's fair to pay (and take) a little less.

You Can't Be All Things to All People

On a drive across Kansas one sunny afternoon, I was listening to a motivational real estate tape in my car. The format consisted of agents calling in with anecdotes, questions and helpful tidbits. This day the topic was handling referrals. One of the callers asked the question: "What do I do if I get referrals for buyers looking for homes that are outside of my area of expertise?"

I was stunned by the moderator's answer which was (in effect)...

"You must qualify the buyer before you waste *your* (emphasis mine) time driving all over the countryside with him. If you're going to drive an hour or more away from home, that buyer better be a real buyer, not just someone kicking tires."

TIRADE ALERT!

Now hold on just a minute. Waste your time? How about the buyer's valuable time? What business does this agent have taking on a buyer outside of her "area of expertise"? When I hire a real estate agent, it's because she is the local expert. She knows the nuances of the neighborhoods, the local market trends. She can tell me if a home is a good deal or if it's overpriced, or if there is a gas station being built on the corner. No matter how good you are, if you don't know the market, you have no business selling homes there. In fact, even as an experienced real estate agent, I always hire a local real estate agent when I buy property outside of Denver.

If you agree to take on a buyer who is looking for homes outside your area, will you be willing to race out every time a new listing comes up, and, as a corollary, will you be tempted to push your buyers to purchase something on your first or second trip just so you don't have to make the drive again? That isn't fair to your buyers. In my humble opinion, agents do a serious disservice to their clients by agreeing to work in an area that they are unfamiliar with.

I recently purchased a few homes in L.A. (Lower Alabama) and talked with four real estate agents prior to selecting one to work with. The first agent I spoke with was referred to me by a friend, and admitted she was not an expert in the area I was considering. I was uneasy about this because I didn't know anything about the area either and wanted an expert to show me around. When she made the comment, "Well, we can learn about Dothan together," I knew I needed to find help elsewhere. Please be fair to your prospects. If you're not the expert, refer them to someone who is. A 25% referral fee for making a phone call sounds like a pretty good deal to me!

The Story of Three Great Real Estate Agents

I've had the privilege of being represented by three great agents in my personal real estate transactions. I'd like to give them public kudos here, and describe what, in my opinion, made them outstanding.

Joan Hart in Steamboat Springs, Colorado; Millie Miller in Dothan, Alabama and Nicole Lincoln in Houston, Texas.

It's an eye-opening experience for real estate professionals to hire other real estate professionals to represent them in a sale or purchase of property. Even if you don't want investment property in other locations, it's almost worth going through the process just to remind yourself what it's like to be so dependent on your real estate agent. You'll come away from the experience with a renewed commitment to look after the needs and protect the vulnerabilities of your own clients.

As I describe why I'm so crazy about these three agents, the word that comes to mind is, again, respect. All three of them respected me as a client, aside even from being a fellow real estate broker. They honored my wishes, considered my opinions, respectfully answered my "silly" questions. At no time did they ever question my judgment or make me feel like a nuisance. And believe me, I can be as annoying and demanding as any other out-of-town buyer! They all made me feel that I was their most important client; I had their complete attention when I needed it.

A Great Listing Agent...

Joan sold an investment townhouse that I purchased pre-construction and eventually flipped for a $30,000 profit. It was a complicated sale. We marketed and sold the townhouse prior to completion, so not only did she get to handle the listing side of the transaction, she also ended up coordinating with the builder on many of the construction details that I probably should have handled, as the original purchaser. When the completion date of the townhouse was delayed...and delayed...and delayed again, she kept everyone calm and committed to the deal. Even being the control freak that I am, at no time did I feel the need to intervene and take over - in fact, the reason I let Joan handle so many details that were probably my responsibility was because she was doing a better job than I would have! Ouch!

And, for the privilege of doing both her job and mine, she cheerfully paid me a 25% referral fee for my business.

A Great Buyer Agent...

Millie helped me buy three houses in Alabama. Even though Millie is one of the top agents in her city, I had her full attention during my first visit to the area.

I told Millie that I "must-have" four bedrooms, a two-car garage and high-speed Internet. She showed me 15 homes in one day. One of them was priced $100,000 higher than the rest, but Millie thought it was an excellent investment and knew that I, as a real estate agent, would probably be interested. She was right. It was a great investment and met all my needs for a personal home in the interim. It needed just the right amount of work and was a perfect "paint and carpet" fix-n-flip. After our long day, it was my number one choice.

I told Millie I was ready to make an offer on the house. I figured she'd be excited about writing up my offer since the home was the most expensive one we'd looked by. Ka-ching for her! But she seemed reluctant to sell it to me. Nonetheless, I insisted and we made an appointment to write the offer on her listing the next day.

A few hours after we parted ways for the day, Millie called me to tell me about a listing she hadn't shown me because it only had three bedrooms. But after spending the day with me, she felt that it might just be The One. And she was right. The minute I drove on to the four acre property in the woods, I was hooked. I don't think I've ever responded so emotionally to a home before. Where was the garage? No garage. High-speed Internet? Nope. Dial-up only. But Millie had seen how I had responded to other homes-in-the-country earlier and realized that a home-in-the-country was what I really wanted. So she found it for me even though I'd told her I was satisfied with and ready to buy the more expensive home in town. She even offered to pay me a referral fee; I didn't even ask. Cool.

A Great Buyer Agent for the Out-of-Town Investor (Me)

A few years ago, I attempted to buy an investment home in the Wilmington, North Carolina area. Nicole Lincoln, who was at Prudential Carolina at the time, was my real estate agent. I found her on the web - in fact, she was the only agent out of the five I e-mailed who responded to me. And I'm so glad she did. Nicole made me feel like her top priority during my visit and was always willing and able to switch gears when I found something new I wanted to explore.

I made an offer on a home three blocks from the ocean. She didn't bat an eye when I wanted to make a lowball offer or when I insisted on including all kinds of additional provisions in the contract that I felt were lacking in the standard North Carolina document. All in all, my offer was rather obnoxious. But she supported me 100% and never made me feel as if I was doing anything remotely inappropriate.

After some back and forth negotiation, I put the home under contract and returned home to Denver. Unfortunately, the home failed the inspection miserably and I terminated the contract under my inspection rights. Again, Nicole supported me 100% and never implied with word or tone that she was disappointed that I'd "wasted" so much of her time. If she was at all annoyed with me, she never let it show. That's class.

Nicole now works in Houston, Texas and I know she'll be wildly successful.

So...thanks Joan, Millie and Nicole! (If you'd like to contact any of my favorite real estate agents, just send me an e-mail at Jennifer@sellwithsoul.com and I'll hook you up.)

Your Guardian Angel

I once listed a 1930's Tudor home for a friend of mine. It was adorable, showed reasonably well, lots of square footage for the money. My friend, the seller, told me that the sewer line had been replaced before she purchased the home, and I took her at her word. That's what she was told, and I didn't ask for any evidence. So, we advertised the home with a newer sewer line. The home didn't sell. And didn't sell. And didn't sell some more. My seller ran out of time, patience and money, so she terminated the listing and rented out the house.

One week after her renter moved in, my seller received a frantic phone call from the tenant that the sewer was backing up in the basement and had flooded everything. Turns out that the sewer line had never been replaced; it was the original clay line and was broken in several places. Either my seller was lied to when she purchased the home or she misunderstood a conversation; either way, she now had a very expensive and disruptive problem on her hands. Not to mention an angry tenant whose belongings had been damaged and was without sewer service for several days!

The moral of the story is twofold. First, when listing a property, always get evidence of repairs made, especially for items like sewer lines that are not visible to a buyer or his inspector. When you are working as a buyer agent, always request documentation of any high-ticket repairs made, so that your client is not blindsided the way my seller was when they go to sell.

But the real reason I tell you this story is this...throughout my real estate career, I have always felt a divine protection over my business. Other agents I have spoken with feel it too. Call it what you will - God, a guardian angel, whatever, but hopefully you will be blessed with one too.

The guardian angel protects you in your first year by allowing challenges no tougher than you can handle; sure, you'll have some painful moments and you'll open your checkbook more than once, but you will be able to resolve most of the issues that arise, even as a beginner. As you become more knowledgeable and creative throughout your career, you will no doubt notice that the degree of difficulty of the real estate problems you encounter seems to increase with your growing competency!

My guardian angel continues to protect me in ways that sure don't seem like "protection." Specifically in not letting perfectly good listings sell. Let me explain.

Many times during my career, I have confidently listed a property at a good price and then watched it languish on the market for no apparent reason. Other similar homes are selling all around my listing, my seller is getting frustrated and both of us are mystified. We bury a St. Christopher statue in the yard, put three pennies under the welcome mat (a Feng Shui trick), and, of course, try price reductions, open houses, newspaper ads, etc. All to no avail. No offers, no real interest.

In the above example with the broken sewer line, let's pretend that the home did sell, and to make it more fun - let's assume the buyer was an attorney. Or married to one.

When that sewer line backed up into the basement after closing, who do you think would have gotten that first frantic phone call? My seller? Nope, me. Guess who's fault this whole mess would have been? My seller's? No again, mine. As a seller's agent, I advertised the home with a new sewer line and could easily have been held liable to make good on my advertising. In other words, I might have had to pay to have the sewer line replaced, as well as cover damage to the new owner's belongings. Sure, my seller would have some liability too, but I'm sure you can see how this situation would be ugly for me.

So, I believe my guardian angel protected me by not allowing the home to sell. As frustrating as it was for all of us, it was a good lesson. One I have learned again and again. In nearly all situations where a good listing isn't selling, we later discover the reason why...either the seller's situation changed and the sale of the home would have been disastrous for them personally, there were latent defects that appeared after the listing was withdrawn, or there was some problem in the home that had to be fixed before it would be "allowed" to sell.

I once marketed and eventually sold a house that had been rebuilt after a significant fire. The home was a 1950's ranch-style home in a marginal neighborhood. Because the insurance company completely restored the home after the fire, it was the most updated home available in the neighborhood. Brand new kitchen, new baths, new windows, new roof, new systems, new plumbing. Most homes in the neighborhood had not been updated and showed poorly. My seller was willing to price the home competitively and I expected it to fly off the market with multiple offers.

It did not. In fact, we went two months without a single showing. In an active market. I was stunned. No amount of advertising seemed to generate any additional interest. We lowered the price several times with no effect. The home was now thousands under market value and still no interest.

One day I stopped by the house for my weekly Fluff & Flush visit and noticed a strong smoke smell permeating the home that hadn't been there before. I thought it was odd, but, to be honest with you, hoped it was my imagination and that it would go away. I went back to the house the following week and the smell was worse. I notified my sellers (who lived out of state) of the problem and they authorized me to hire a company who specialized in removing odors from homes. After three attempts to remove the smell, the odor-eliminator company admitted defeat.

To cut to the chase, it turned out that one burned stud in a bedroom wall had not been replaced in the restoration of the home, and in the heat of the summer, the charred wood started to smell. The contractor who did the work replaced the stud and the smell went away entirely. Within four days, we had seven showings and a full price offer.

I knew it was my guardian angel protecting me from selling the home. Until we solved the problem, that home was going to sit there. Now, whenever I have a listing that is inexplicably not selling, I describe the guardian angel phenomenon to my seller and ask him to open his mind to potential issues that might be holding back the sale of his home.

Ya Do What Ya Gotta Do...

There are times in real estate (lots of 'em) when you will go above and beyond the call of duty (in your humble opinion) in order to please your client, secure your paycheck or simply because it's the right thing to do. As you gain experience, these "opportunities" will appear to lessen, but perhaps only because you now realize they are part of your job, or you've gotten better at delegating such duties back to your client...who probably should have taken care of them in the first place.

For example, what if you show up to do an open house, fresh cookies and sign-in sheets in hand...and the beds are unmade? You probably won't discover this until your seller has left, or if you do notice it, you might not have the guts to say anything - after all, if the seller doesn't care, why should you? But hopefully you do care, so go make the beds. Sure, I know you'd really rather not, but do it anyway.

Or what about that $800,000 spec home listing you have with the dusty contractor footprints across the "gleaming" Brazilian cherry floors? I can't tell you how many times I've mopped the floors of my listings to make sure they show their best. How about the lawn of a vacant listing that is dying due to lack of water? Yes, I have spent all afternoon watering my client's yard. Just sat in the house with my cell phone and a good book, moving the sprinkler around every 20 minutes or so. I once had a cleaning "party" with the listing agent of a condo my buyers were closing on later that day. Three hours prior to the closing, we could be found in rubber gloves scrubbing toilets, dusting ceiling fans, cleaning baseboards.

Yeah, real estate is so glamorous. Once I waited in the alley at 7:00 a.m. for the garbage truck. My buyer client was under contract to purchase an older home (1920's vintage) with a one-car detached garage that was entered from the alley (typical in old Denver). However, a Denver city dumpster sat directly across the alley from the garage door, which made entry into the garage impossible. There wasn't enough room to make the turn. I called the Denver Waste Management Department and asked them to move the dumpster so my client could access his garage. They told me the only way to ensure the relocation of the dumpster was to catch the trash men on trash day. So there I was, standing in an alley, morning coffee in hand, waiting for the garbage truck to come through.

Once I painted the interior of a house for my client. Would I do that again? Uh, no. It was a ridiculous thing for me to do - my clients were not destitute, far from it, and they certainly could have hired a professional painter. But I was enthusiastic and, for some crazy reason, it seemed like a good idea at the time. My enthusiasm must have been contagious because I even got my assistant to help me!

Anyway, this good deed ended up being worth doing. When my sellers told their friends, Darren and Samantha, about my painting "service," they were so impressed they hired me to sell their $400,000 home and be the buyer agent on their replacement $600,000 home! So, in reality, I was paid over $20,000 for my painting efforts. I can't promise this will happen to you every time, but you never know.

If It Feels Wrong, Don't Do It

Sometimes you'll be presented with a deal that feels good, but just doesn't feel right. Maybe you feel that you're taking advantage of a situation or that you're getting a paycheck you really don't deserve. Other agents tell you to take the money and run - after all, there are plenty of times you work hard and don't get paid for it. But that little voice inside you is telling you different.

I worked with a client who wanted to buy a piece of property on which to build a custom home. To be clear, this was not a home in a new subdivision, it was just a buildable lot on the outskirts of town. The lot was around $100,000; the home he wanted to build would be around $500,000. I found him the lot and put it under contract. He went out and found a general contractor to build him his custom home. Apparently, it is common practice for the real estate agent to get paid a commission on the final price of the home, even though my involvement with the construction of the home was nil. Nada. I certainly wasn't going to negotiate the cost of lumber or otherwise involve myself in the building process. Even my buyer seemed okay with paying me on the final price, but it just felt wrong.

Following my conscience, I declined to assert my "right" to a commission on the construction of his home and just took a fee on the purchase of the lot. I wish I could say that my ethical behavior resulted in a flood of referrals from my buyer, but it didn't really. I feel good about it anyway. That's enough.

Another time I agreed to facilitate a sale between related parties. A woman bought her brother's house and asked me to put the paperwork together. We agreed on a fee of $1,000 for my real estate services. I prepared the contract, explained it to both parties, and delivered the contract to the lender and title company. All in all, it took me two hours, tops. Since it was a friendly transaction, there was no inspection to negotiate and no other problems arose. The loan went through smoothly and as it turned out, I couldn't even attend the closing because I was out of town. I felt guilty accepting the $1,000 fee for two hours work, so I returned it. I just didn't feel right charging $500/hour for something that was so easy for me to do.

Show some respect and empathy for your clients. At the least, try not to embarrass yourself and the industry by gouging people whenever the opportunity presents itself. Maybe they won't complain to your face, but believe me, they notice. People aren't stupid and they aren't gullible. You might get their money, but it's never worth it if the real cost is your self-respect, or if you don't care about that, your reputation in the community.

Don't get me wrong, you do work for free a lot and deserve nice paychecks for your efforts. But that isn't a blank check to overcharge people unfairly. They may not even openly balk at your fee, but it wouldn't hurt to "take advantage" of the opportunity to do a good deed and improve the reputation of the real estate community!

TO WRAP UP - A FEW WORDS OF ENCOURAGEMENT

Do you ever look at the Sunday real estate section of the newspaper and see all those smiling faces looking out at you? All that competition? I did when I was new and it was quite intimidating. So many real estate agents, all with more experience and expertise than I had - how was I ever going to break into the business? Surely all my friends already knew five or six agents who had been serving their family for generations...

Surprise, they probably don't! The vast majority of your friends and acquaintances have no real loyalty to any real estate agent. They'll be happy to work with you if you ask for their business. And this is one place the public's lack of appreciation for the real estate industry can work for you! Since real estate looks so easy, many times your inexperience won't be a factor if your friends consider you a reasonably competent human being. They think real estate agents just hold open houses and drive buyers around and, in the beginning, let 'em think that. They may not be too concerned about finding someone more experienced...after all, how hard can it be? Of course, when you have a few years under your belt, you will certainly use your experience to your advantage when competing against a freshman agent who is a friend of the family, but as a rookie, don't fret about it too much.

There is plenty of business out there, there really is. If you can sell 20 homes a year, you should be able to pay the bills. That's only 20 people out of your whole town who have to hire you. Just because you're new doesn't mean that you have to start at the bottom. You are not lined up behind all those smiling faces in the Sunday paper. You can jump right in and see them next year at the Board of Realtors® annual awards luncheon.

Question Convention

As you go through your first year, you will get a lot of advice from your broker, other agents, teachers and trainers. If something doesn't sound right to you, don't assume it is. Real estate is full of interesting (and some not-so) characters who don't deserve the benefit of the doubt just because they have more experience than you do. I ignored almost all of the advice I got through the years. Real estate is full of gray areas and you can almost always find multiple solutions to the problems you face. Don't be afraid to go with your gut instinct. If you're selling with soul, I can guarantee that you won't regret it.

Random Reflections
So, what do I mean by "An Extraordinary Career?"

Ah, I'm glad you asked me that. But first, let me ask you...what do you think I mean? Or, in other words, what would make a career "extraordinary" for you?

Clearly, "extraordinary" means different things to different people. To some, it means making gobs and gobs of money, and that's nothing to be ashamed of. And, by the way, entirely possible in real estate. To others, it means having a career that makes you want to jump out of bed in the morning and get started (and making gobs and gobs of money). Some would consider their career extraordinary if it helped them help others. How about building a business to pass on to your children? Or a career that allows you the flexibility to travel or spend more time with family? Or to retire early?

A career in real estate offers all of these benefits and more. After ten years in the business, here's what my life looks like - I'm 39 years old and I recently moved to Alabama, where I live on my four-acre "estate" in the country. I go to Mexico or the Caribbean at least three times a year; I could go more often, but I've always loved my job and haven't needed to "get away" from it. I took a sabbatical of sorts three years ago and was able to live comfortably on my savings for six months before I got bored enough to go back to work. I typically own six rental properties at a time and I buy and sell at least three every year, which keeps the dogs fed and gives me a nice petty-cash fund. When I'm working "full-time" I work about five hours a day, eight months of the year. The rest of the time I write, which has been a life-long dream of mine, and real estate has allowed me the luxury of pursuing that dream.

I've never dreaded mornings or Mondays; in fact during the peak of my career, I never took more than a four-day vacation because I truly loved my job... I couldn't stand to be away that long! I am proud of the business I created and while I won't claim that everybody loves me (I got over that fantasy early on), I do believe that I made more people happy than unhappy. And, I helped several of my clients make their own gobs and gobs of money with their real estate investments.

How does all this sound to you? I'm sure you realize that you won't be enjoying such a lifestyle this year or next, but it can happen quicker than you think. And in the meantime, if you're selling with your soul, you *will* enjoy working hard, you *will* be proud of the business you build and yes, you *will* make a comfortable living, perhaps even an extraordinary one.

Your career will be extraordinary if you follow your heart, do what feels natural and work damn hard. Okay, so working damn hard might not feel natural, but you might be surprised how hard you're happy to work when you're thrilled with and proud of what you're doing...

So...best wishes on your real estate career. I hope I've been helpful. Contrary to popular belief (and my own fantasies) most authors do not lead a glamorous life of chatting with Oprah and attending book release bashes. Well, hell, maybe they do, but I don't. Anyway, my point is that I can probably help you out if you want more information on any ideas or suggestions you found in this book. Or, if you want someone to bounce your own outside-the-box ideas off of...drop me a line!

My website is <u>www.SellWithSoul.com</u>. You'll find lots of good information there, including printable versions of my checklists, my full listing presentation template and other samples of client communication, links to my preferred vendors, and anything else I come up with.

Go get 'em.

An Additional Resource...

The companion guide to Sell with Soul is titled *Getting Started and Staying on Track; The What, When, Where, Why and How-to's of Your First Year in Real Estate.* It is part workbook and part fully-loaded survival kit for first-year agents.

Don't worry, you do not need the companion guide to fully benefit from *Sell with Soul*. However, the companion guide goes into additional details I couldn't quite fit in here. I cover topics such as creating your listing presentation template, making your "I'm in Real Estate" announcement, preparing for and holding your first open house and building your team, along with such little details as recording your out-going voicemail message, setting up your communication systems and even whether or not to use the seller's toilet while previewing! I'll help you track your expenses, decide whether or not to work from home and even get ready for your first vacation.

It is available right now, for purchase as an e-book on my website, www.sellwithsoul.com. So, for instance, if your first listing appointment is three days away, you can access this new guide quickly by downloading it. You will find the process of preparing a professional listing presentation outlined in complete detail. Or perhaps you are preparing for your first "real buyer? There's a whole chapter on getting ready for her as well.

The e-book takes you day-by-day through your first three weeks, with daily assignments and weekly follow-up reminders. I'll help you set goals, and better yet, reach them. I want you to have an extraordinary career in real estate. A strong beginning will help ensure that you do.

APPENDIX

Buyer-Under-Contract Checklist

New Listing Checklist

Listing-Under-Contract Checklist

HOA Questionnaire For the Listing Agent

Information Sheet for Condominium Buyers

These checklists, in printable form, are available at www.SellwithSoul.com

BUYER-UNDER-CONTRACT CHECKLIST

ACTIVITY	DUE DATE	√ WHEN COMPLETE
Enter contract dates into contact management program	Day of Contract	
Fax contract to lender	Day of Contract	
Deliver property disclosures to buyer	Day of Contract	
Deliver earnest money to listing agent	Day of Contract	
Give buyer HOA contact information & questionnaire	Day of Contract	
Give buyer inspector names & numbers	Day of Contract	
Call buyer's lender to confirm loan application	1st Week after Contract	
Call buyer's lender to discuss scheduling appraisal	1st Week after Contract	
Deliver signed disclosures to listing agent	1st Week after Contract	
Tell buyer to look into homeowner hazard insurance	1st Week after Contract	
Call buyer's lender to check in	1st Week after Contract	
Has closing been scheduled?	1st Week after Contract	
Is buyer doing a mail-out close or POA?	2nd Week after Contract	
Are the inspection items done?	1 Week before Closing	
Get documentation of inspection repairs	1 Week before Closing	
Schedule walk-thru	1 Week before Closing	
Remind buyer to transfer utilities	1 Week before Closing	
Send any changes to lender and/or title company	2-4 Days before Closing	
Confirm closing time & place	2-4 Days before Closing	
Review closing figures with buyer	2-4 Days before Closing	
Tell buyer to bring driver's license & cashiers check to closing	2-4 Days before Closing	
Prepare the file for closing	Right before Closing	
Turn the file in to the office manager	Right after Closing	
Add buyer to your SOI (or change buyer's address)	Right after Closing	
Add buyer to your post-closing follow-up program	Right after Closing	
Call buyer to check on move	4 Days after Closing	

New Listing Checklist

ACTIVITY	DUE DATE	√ WHEN COMPLETE
Seller signature on all listing contracts & disclosures	Prior to MLS entry	
Take pictures	Prior to MLS entry	
Schedule the Virtual Tour	Day of MLS entry	
Get the key, install the lockbox	Day of MLS entry	
Get HOA contact information from seller	Day of MLS entry	
Enter the listing on MLS	Day of MLS entry	
Enter the listing on your contact manager program	Day of MLS entry	
Order 'Just Listed' cards	Day of MLS entry	
Track the expiration date	Day of MLS entry	
Install the For Sale sign	Day of MLS entry	
Showing information to showing desk/showing service	Day of MLS entry	
Create & display 'Special Features' cards in the home	Day of MLS entry	
Send a copy of the MLS listing to the seller	Day of MLS entry	
Deliver copies of all signed documents to seller	1 Day after MLS entry	
Prepare the home brochure	1 Day after MLS entry	
Schedule open house	1 Day after MLS entry	
Call the HOA to verify information	1st week after MLS entry	
Deliver home brochures to home	When ready	
Solicit feedback, provide to seller	1st week after MLS entry	(Ongoing)
Load Internet advertising	1st week after MLS entry	
Email web links to seller	1st week after MLS entry	
Fluff & Flush 1	7 Days after MLS entry	
First marketing update to seller	7 Days after MLS entry	
Call Seller "Are the showing instructions working for you?"	7 Days after MLS entry	
Fluff & Flush 2	2nd week after MLS entry	
Call seller "Need more brochures yet?"	2nd week after MLS entry	
Fluff & Flush 3 (continue every week)	3rd week after MLS entry	
Call seller "Need more brochures yet?"	3rd week after MLS entry	
Second market update to seller	3rd week after MLS entry	
Prepare & schedule 6 week CMA meeting/ 3rd market update	6th week after MLS entry	
Pick up brochure box	6th week after MLS entry	
Re-do exterior photos?	When season changes	
Fourth market update to seller	8th week after MLS entry	

LISTING-UNDER-CONTRACT CHECKLIST

ACTIVITY	DUE DATE	√ WHEN COMPLETE
Get the earnest money check	Day of Contract	
Turn in contract file to office manager	Day of Contract	
Enter contract dates into your contract manager program	Day of Contract	
Order title work and HOA documents	Day of Contract	
Change the status in the MLS	Day of Contract	
Notify showing desk/showing service of status change	Day of Contract	
Notify agents with showing appointments of status change	Day of Contract	
Send property disclosures to the buyer agent	Day of Contract	
Call buyer's lender and introduce yourself	1st Week after Contract	
Pick up the brochure box	1st Week after Contract	
Get payoff information from seller	1st Week after Contract	
Property disclosures returned from buyer with signature?	1st Week after Contract	
Put up SOLD sign	2nd Week after Contract	
Call buyer's lender	2nd Week after Contract	
Prepare for the appraisal	2nd Week after Contract	
Set the closing	2nd Week after Contract	
Confirm that the inspection items are complete	1 Week before Closing	
Confirm that seller has arranged cleaning	1 Week before Closing	
Arrange mail-out close or POA	1 Week before Closing	
Send any changes to lender and/or title company	1 Week before Closing	
Is the buyer doing a walk-thru?	1 Week before Closing	
Confirm closing time, date & place with all parties	1 Week before Closing	
Review closing figures	1-2 Days before Closing	
Remind seller to bring driver's license to closing	1-2 Days before Closing	
Order earnest money check from office manager	1-2 Days before Closing	
Prepare the file for closing	1-2 Days before Closing	
Pick up the sign, lockbox and interior brochure box	Day of Closing	
Turn in closed file to office manager	Right after Closing	
Notify showing desk/showing service of closed status	Right after Closing	
Add seller to post-closing follow -up plan	1-2 Days after Closing	
Update seller's address in your SOI	1-2 Days after Closing	
Call seller after move-out	3-5 Days after Closing	
Update websites with sale	3-5 Days after Closing	

HOA QUESTIONNAIRE FOR THE LISTING AGENT

Spoke with _____ Date_____

Are there any restrictions on For Sale/Open House signs? _____

What is the monthly management fee? _____

What does it cover?

Heat, Water/Sewer, Insurance, Roof, Pool/Tennis, Snow Removal, Trash

Other? _____

Do you expect it to increase in the near future? _____

What is the transfer fee at sale?_____

How much is the working capital/reserve deposit? _____

Is the working capital/reserve refundable at sale? _____

Are there any special assessments coming up?_____

Is the building/project FHA-approved? _____

Who should an interested buyer contact if they have questions?

Name _____ Phone Number _____

Who do I contact for financials, minutes, etc?

Name _____ Phone Number _____

Any other information, e.g., pet restrictions, upcoming improvements, etc.?

_____

INFORMATION SHEET FOR CONDOMINIUM BUYERS

When you purchase a condominium or townhome, you will automatically belong to the Home Owners Association (HOA). Every HOA is a little different, with individual strengths and weaknesses. It is in your best interest to contact the HOA to judge for yourself if you are comfortable with the fees, the rules and regulations, the financial stability of the association and the way the HOA is organized.

Please call _____
prior to _____ and ask the following questions:

1. What is the monthly management fee and what does it cover?

2. Are there any planned or contemplated special assessments coming up?

3. Do you have a "working capital" deposit required of new homeowners? How much is it? Is it refundable on sale?

4. Do you have any restrictions, e.g., pets, children, smoking, that I should be aware of?

5. Are you planning to make any improvements to the property in the near future?

6. Are there any special move-in procedures or costs I need to know about?

7. Is there anything else a potential buyer of the property should know?

Depending on the property, you may also want to ask about the age of the heating system and roof, guest parking, barbecue grill restrictions, etc.

I acknowledge that I have been given this Condominium Buyer Information Sheet by _____ of _____, and agree to contact the Home Owners Association with any questions or concerns I may have about the HOA and/or the project itself.

_____   _____
Buyer   Date

_____   _____
Buyer   Date

Printed in the United States
114538LV00003B/329/A

9 781425 968816